麦格希 **中英双语阅读文库**

# 真假珍珠

## 美国名人短篇小说精选

# 第2辑

【美】德雷伯 (C. G. Draper) ●主编

李晓东 ●译

麦格希中英双语阅读文库编委会 ●编

全国百佳图书出版单位
吉林出版集团股份有限公司

图书在版编目（CIP）数据

美国名人短篇小说精选. 第2辑, 真假珍珠 / (美)
德雷伯(C．G．Draper) 主编；李晓东译；麦格希中英
双语阅读文库编委会编. -- 2版. -- 长春：吉林出版
集团股份有限公司, 2018.3（2022.1重印）
（麦格希中英双语阅读文库）
ISBN 978-7-5581-4744-9

Ⅰ.①美… Ⅱ.①德… ②李… ③麦… Ⅲ.①英语—
汉语—对照读物②短篇小说—小说集—美国 Ⅳ.
①H319.4：I

中国版本图书馆CIP数据核字(2018)第046059号

## 美国名人短篇小说精选 第2辑 真假珍珠

编：麦格希中英双语阅读文库编委会
插　画：齐　航　李延霞
责任编辑：朱　玲
封面设计：冯冯翼
开　本：660mm×960mm　1/16
字　数：231千字
印　张：10.25
版　次：2018年3月第2版
印　次：2022年1月第2次印刷

出　版：吉林出版集团股份有限公司
发　行：吉林出版集团外语教育有限公司
地　址：长春市福祉大路5788号龙腾国际大厦B座7层
　　　　邮编：130011
电　话：总编办：0431-81629929
　　　　发行部：0431-81629927　0431-81629921(Fax)
印　刷：北京一鑫印务有限责任公司

ISBN 978-7-5581-4744-9　　　定价：38.00元
版权所有　　侵权必究　　举报电话：0431-81629929

# 前 言 *PREFACE*

英国思想家培根说过：阅读使人深刻。阅读的真正目的是获取信息，开拓视野和陶冶情操。从语言学习的角度来说，学习语言若没有大量阅读就如隔靴搔痒，因为阅读中的语言是最丰富、最灵活、最具表现力、最符合生活情景的，同时读物中的情节、故事引人入胜，进而能充分调动读者的阅读兴趣，培养读者的文学修养，至此，语言的学习水到渠成。

"麦格希中英双语阅读文库"在世界范围内选材，涉及科普、社会文化、文学名著、传奇故事、成长励志等多个系列，充分满足英语学习者课外阅读之所需，在阅读中学习英语、提高能力。

◎难度适中

本套图书充分照顾读者的英语学习阶段和水平，从读者的阅读兴趣出发，以难易适中的英语语言为立足点，选材精心、编排合理。

◎精品荟萃

本套图书注重经典阅读与实用阅读并举。既包含国内外脍炙人口、耳熟能详的美文，又包含科普、人文、故事、励志类等多学科的精彩文章。

◎功能实用

本套图书充分体现了双语阅读的功能和优势，充分考虑到读者课外阅读的方便，超出核心词表的词汇均出现在使其意义明显的语境之中，并标注释义。

鉴于编者水平有限，凡不周之处，谬误之处，皆欢迎批评教正。

我们真心地希望本套图书承载的文化知识和英语阅读的策略对提高读者的英语著作欣赏水平和英语运用能力有所裨益。

丛书编委会

# Contents

*A Jury of Her Peers*

*April Showers*

# 01

# A Jury of Her Peers

Adapted from the story by Susan Glaspell

Susan Glaspell was born in 1882, in Davenport, Iowa. She worked for a newspaper there until she earned enough to support herself by writing *fiction*. She wrote a lot—ten novels and more than forty stories. But she is also well known for her *plays*. She and her husband *founded* a famous theater, the Provincetown Playhouse, in Provincetown, Massachusetts (on Cape Cod), in 1915. Her husband *directed* plays by young, unknown writers. Many of these writers later became famous. Glaspell first wrote "A Jury of Her Peers" as a play

## 她的同性陪审团

根据苏珊·格拉斯佩尔的同名故事改写

苏珊·格拉斯佩尔1882年生于爱荷华州达文波特市。她最初在一家报社工作，有了一定的经济基础后就开始从事文学创作。作品涵盖十部小说、四十多篇短篇故事。但是她以戏剧而闻名。1915年，她与丈夫在马萨诸塞州的普林斯顿创建了普林斯顿剧院。她的丈夫导演了一些年轻的不知名作家的话剧。后来其中许多作家出名了。格拉斯佩尔最初创作的"她的同性陪审团"是一部戏剧，名为《琐事》，trifles这个

fiction *n.* 小说　　　　　　　　　　　play *n.* 剧本；戏剧
found *v.* 建立　　　　　　　　　　　direct *v.* 导演

# A Jury of Her Peers

called *Trifles*—the word means "small things of little value." Later, she rewrote the play as a story. Glaspell often wrote about people trapped by the choices they make in life. She died in 1948.

I

Martha Hale opened the storm door and felt the cutting north wind. She ran back inside for her big wool *shawl*. She was unhappy with what she saw there in her kitchen. Her bread was all ready for mixing, half the *flour sifted* and half unsifted. She hated to see things half done. But it was no ordinary thing that called her away. It was probably further from ordinary than anything that had ever happened in Dickson County.

She had been sifting flour when the *sheriff* drove up with his horse and buggy to get Mr. Hale. Sheriff Peters had asked Mrs. Hale to

---

词义为"微不足道的小事"。后来她又将其改写为短篇小说。她的写作对象常常是由于错误抉择而陷入人生困境的人物。格拉斯佩尔逝世于1948年。

I

一推开外面的防风门,玛撒·黑尔便感受到了北风的刺骨,她赶紧跑回屋去拿大羊毛披肩。经过厨房时看到的一幕让她不快。她正准备和面做面包,面粉已经筛出来一半,还有一半没筛呢。她平时可容不得这样,什么事非得做完才罢休。然而今天却是万不得已,因为发生了一件非同寻常的事,可能比以往任何一件发生在迪克森郡的事情都更加非同寻常。

警长驾着马车来接黑尔先生时,她正在筛面粉。彼得斯警长又请黑

---

shawl *n.* 围巾
sift *v.* 筛(某物)

flour *n.* 面粉
sheriff *n.* 行政长官

come, too. His wife was nervous, he said with a *grin*. She wanted another woman to come along. So Martha Hale had dropped everything right where it was.

"Martha!" her husband's voice came, "don't keep the *folks* waiting out here in the cold!"

She tied the wool shawl tighter and climbed into the *buggy*. Three men and a woman were waiting for her. Martha Hale had met Mrs. Peters, the sheriff's wife, at the county *fair*. Mrs. Peters didn't seem like a sheriff's wife. She was small and thin and ordinary. She didn't have a strong voice. But Mr. Peter certainly did look like a sheriff. He was a heavy man with a big voice, very friendly to folks who followed the law. But now, Mrs. Hale thought, he was going to the Wrights' house as a sheriff, not a friend.

---

尔夫人一同前往，他笑了笑，说自己的妻子太紧张了，想要个女伴。就这样，玛撒·黑尔就不得不把手头儿的活放下跟着去了。

"玛撒！"她听到丈夫在喊，"外边太冷，别让大伙儿等起来没完！"

她系紧羊毛披肩，上了车。车上有三男一女在等着她。玛撒·黑尔以前在集市上见过警长太太彼得斯夫人，她长得又瘦又小，相貌平淡无奇，说话柔声细语，怎么看也不像警长太太。但彼得斯先生看上去却很像个地道的警长：大块头，大嗓门，对遵纪守法的百姓非常友善。可他此行去赖特家，却是作为一个警长，而不是朋友，黑尔夫人心想。

---

grin *n.* 露齿笑  
buggy *n.* 轻便马车

folk *n.* 人们  
fair *n.* 集市

The Wrights' house looked lonely this cold March morning. It had always been a lonely-looking house. It was down in a *valley*, and the *poplar* trees around it were lonely-looking trees. The men were talking about what had happened there: her husband, Sheriff Peters, and the county *attorney*, Mr. Henderson. She looked over at Mrs. Peters.

"I'm glad you came with me," Mrs. Peters said nervously.

When the buggy reached the *doorstep*, Martha Hale felt she could not go inside. She had often said to herself, "I must go over and see Minnie Foster." She still thought of her as Minnie Foster, though for twenty years she had been Mrs. Wright. But there was always something to do, and Minnie Foster would go from her mind. She felt sad that she had come only now.

---

赖特家的房屋在三月份这个寒冷的清晨显得孤寂而冷清。房屋位于谷底，总是给人一种孤寂而冷清的感觉，四周的白杨树也是同样的孤寂和冷清。三个男人——黑尔先生，彼得斯警长，郡里的律师亨得森先生——在谈论这里发生的事。黑尔夫人则看着那边的彼得斯夫人。

"我很高兴你能陪我一起来，"彼得斯夫人说话的时候有点紧张。

马车到了门口，玛撒·黑尔却不想进去。她常常对自己说："我得去看看明妮·福斯特了。"尽管明妮·福斯特二十年前就已成为赖特夫人，可黑尔夫人总觉得她还是明妮·福斯特。想归想，手头却总有忙不完的事，去看明妮的事也就罢了。就这样一直拖到今天才来，黑尔夫人不禁感

---

valley  n.  山谷
attorney  n.  律师

poplar  n.  白杨；白杨木
doorstep  n.  门阶

The men went over to stand by the *stove*. The women stood together by the door. At first, they didn't even look around the *kitchen*.

"Now, Mr. Hale," the sheriff began. "Before we move things around, you tell Mr. Henderson what you saw when you came here yesterday morning."

Ⅱ

Mrs. Hale felt nervous for her husband. Lewis Hale often lost his way in a story. She hoped he would tell it straight this time. *Unnecessary* things would just make it harder for Minnie Foster.

"Yes, Mr. Hale?" the *county* attorney said.

---

到悲伤。

男人们走进去，站到了炉边，两个女人则站在门口。刚开始，他们甚至都没有到厨房看看。

"好了，黑尔先生，"警长开始说话了。"在移动现场的东西之前，你跟亨得森先生说说昨天一早来都看到了什么。"

Ⅱ

黑尔夫人不太放心她的丈夫——刘易斯·黑尔说起什么事来经常颠三倒四。她希望这次他能直截了当一些，无关的情节只会对明妮·福斯特更为不利。

"说吧，黑尔先生？"郡律师说道。

---

stove *n.* 火炉　　　　　　　　　　kitchen *n.* 厨房
unnecessary *adj.* 不必要的　　　　county *n.* 郡；县

"I started to town with *a load of* potatoes," Mrs. Hale's husband began. "I came along this road, and I saw the house. I said to myself, 'I'm going to see John Wright about the telephone.' They will bring a telephone out here if I can get somebody else to help pay for it. I'd spoken to Wright before, but he said folks talked too much already. All he asked for was *peace* and quiet. I guess you know how much he talked himself. But I thought I would ask him in front of his wife. All the women like the telephone. In this *lonely* road it would be a good thing. Not that he cared much about what his wife wanted..."

Now there he was!—saying things he didn't need to say. Mrs. Hale tried to catch her husband's eye, but luckily the attorney *interrupted* him with:

---

"我拉着一些土豆进城，"她的丈夫开始说："我沿着这条路走，我看见了这座房子。我自言自语地说，'我得去看看约翰·赖特，谈谈电话的事。'要是再能找出一个人来合伙出钱的话，这儿就能安上电话了。以前就和赖特谈过这事，可他说人们眼下尽说空话，除了平和、宁静的生活，他什么也不想要。我猜你们肯定知道他一个人啰啰嗦嗦地说了多久。这次我想当着他妻子的面问问他。女人都喜欢电话。在这条偏僻的公路上安个电话可是件好事。倒不是他有多在乎他妻子的要求……"

又来了！——又说没用的事儿。黑尔夫人很想用目光暗示丈夫，好在律师用下面的话打断了他：

---

a load of 大量；许多　　　　　　　　peace *n.* 和平
lonely *adj.* 偏僻的　　　　　　　　interrupt *v.* 打断；中断

"Just tell what happened when you got there, Mr. Hale."

Mr. Hale began again, more *carefully*. "I *knocked* at the door. But it was all quiet inside. I knew they must be up—it was past eight o'clock. I knocked again, louder, and I thought I heard someone say, 'Come in.' I opened the door—this door"—Mr. Hale pointed toward the door where the two women stood. "And there, in that *rocking chair*"—he pointed to it—"sat Mrs. Wright."

"How did she look?" the county attorney asked.

"Well," said Hale, "she looked—strange."

"How do you mean—strange?"

The attorney took out a notebook and pencil. Mrs. Hale did not like that pencil. She kept her eye on her husband, as if to tell him,

---

"说说你来的时候都发生了什么就行了，黑尔先生。"

黑尔先生重新开始，这次更谨慎了。"我敲了敲门。可是里面一点儿声音也没有。我知道他们肯定都起来了——已经八点多了。我又使劲敲了敲门，觉得里面有人说：'进来。'我打开门——就是这扇门"——黑尔先生指了指两位女人站立的地方。"就在那儿，就在那把摇椅上"——他又指了指那把摇椅——"赖特太太就坐在那儿。"

"当时她看起来怎么样？"律师问。

"哦，"黑尔说："她看起来——很怪。"

"你是什么意思——怎么个怪法？"

律师拿出笔记本和铅笔，那铅笔可不太招黑尔夫人喜欢。她盯着丈夫，看样子是在告诫他："别说废话，说出来记到本子上就是麻烦。"黑

---

carefully *adv.* 小心地　　　　　　　　　　　　　　　knock *v.* 敲
rocking chair 摇椅

"No unnecessary things. They'll just go into that notebook and *make trouble*." Hale spoke carefully, as if the pencil made him think more slowly.

"Well, she didn't seem to know what she was going to do next. I said, 'How do, Mrs. Wright. It's cold isn't it?' And she said, 'Is it?,' and sat there *fingering* her *apron*, nervous—like."

"Well, I was surprised. She didn't ask me to come in and sit down, but just sat there, not even looking at me. And so I said, 'I want to see John.'"

"And then she laughed—I guess you'd call it a laugh."

"I said, a little sharp, 'Can I see John?'"

---

尔先生字斟句酌，就好像是那支铅笔让他的思维减慢了似的。

"嗯，她好像有点魂不守舍。我说：'早啊，赖特夫人，今儿天真冷啊！'她说：'是吗？'她坐在那儿光是摆弄围裙，样子挺紧张。"

"我呢，觉得很吃惊。她既没让我进屋，也没让我坐下。光是坐在那儿，连看都不看我一眼。我只好说：'我要见见约翰。'"

"这时，她居然哈哈大笑起来——我想应该叫'大笑'"。

"我提高了嗓门，又说，'我可以见见约翰吗？'"

---

make trouble 制造麻烦　　　　　　finger *v.* 用手指拨弄
apron *n.* 围裙

"'No,' she said, kind of dull. 'Isn't he home?' I said. 'Yes,' says she, 'he's home.' 'Then why can't I see him?' I asked her. Now I was angry. 'Because he's dead,' says she—all quiet and *dull*. She fingered her apron some more."

"'Why, where is he?' I said, not knowing what to say.

"She just *pointed* upstairs—like this," said Hale, pointing. "Then I said, 'Why, what did he die of?'"

"'He died of a *rope* around his neck,' says she, and just went on fingering her apron."

Nobody spoke. Everyone looked at the rockingchair as if they saw the woman who had sat there yesterday.

---

"'不'，她有点麻木地说。'他不在家吗？'我问。'在啊，'她说，'他在家。'我有点生气，又问：'那我为什么不能见他？''因为他死了，'她说这话的时候显得挺平静，没什么表情，手里还摆弄着围裙。"

"'什么，他在哪儿？'我问，我当时实在不知道该说什么好了。"

"她指了指楼上——就像这样，"黑尔边说边指了指楼上。我接着问：'他是怎么死的？'"

"'用绳子勒死的，'她一边说，一边接着摆弄围裙。"

没人说什么话。每个人都看着那张摇椅，就好像看到了昨天还坐在上面的女人。

---

dull  *adj.*  无趣的；呆滞的                              point  *v.*  指向
rope  *n.*  绳；绳索

"And what did you do then?" The attorney at last interrupted the *silence*.

"I went upstairs." Hale's voice fell. "There he was—lying on the—he was dead, all right. I thought I'd better not *touch* anything. So I went downstairs.

"'Who did this, Mrs. Wright?' I said, sharp, and she stops fingering her apron. 'I don't know,' she says. 'You don't know?' said I. 'Weren't you sleeping in the same bed with him? Somebody tied a rope around his neck and killed him, and you didn't *wake up*?'"

"'I didn't wake up,' she says after me."

"I may have looked as if I didn't see how that could be. After a minute she said, 'I sleep sound.'"

"那你又做了些什么？"最后是律师打破了沉默。

"我上楼了，"黑尔压低了声音说。"他就在那儿，躺着——真的死了。我想最好什么也别碰，所以，我又下楼了。"

"'这是谁干的，赖特太太？'我厉声问。她停下来，不再摆弄围裙。'不知道，'她回答说。'你不知道？'我说。'你不是和他睡在一张床上吗？有人把绳子勒在他脖子上，杀了他，你居然没醒？'"

"'我没醒，'她紧接着说。"

"我当时可能满脸愕然的样子。过了一会儿，她又说，'我睡得太死了。'"

silence *n.* 沉默；寂静　　　　　touch *v.* 触摸
wake up 醒来

"I thought maybe she *ought to* tell her story first to the sheriff. So I went as fast as I could to the nearest telephone—over at the Rivers' place on High Road. Then I came back here to wait for Sheriff Peters."

"I thought I should talk to her. So I said I had stopped by to see if John wanted to put in a telephone. At that, she started to laugh, and then she stopped and looked frightened..."

The attorney spoke to the sheriff. "I *guess* we'll go upstairs first—then out to the *barn* and around there. You made sure yesterday that there's nothing important here in the kitchen?"

"Nothing here but kitchen things," said the sheriff with a laugh.

The attorney was searching in the *cupboard*. After a minute he

---

"我觉得这事儿她应该先和警长说清楚，所以就用最快的速度找到了最近的电话，就是河边公路上的那一部。打了电话之后，就回来等彼得斯警长。"

"我想应该和她聊聊，所以就跟她讲我是顺便来看看约翰是否愿意装一部电话的。刚说到这儿，她就开始哈哈大笑，笑着笑着突然又停了下来，一副很害怕的样子……"

律师对警长说："我想我们应该先上楼看看，然后看看谷仓，再四处转转。你昨天能拿准厨房里没有什么重要的情况吗？"

"没有，都是些厨房用的家什，"警长笑着说。

律师把手伸进碗橱里摸索起来，过了一会儿，他把手抽出来，上面沾

---

ought to  *应该*

barn  *n.*  谷仓

guess  *v.*  猜测

cupboard  *n.*  碗柜

pulled out his hand, all *sticky*.

"Here's a nice *mess*," he said angrily.

"Oh—her fruit," Mrs. Peters said. She looked at Mrs. Hale. "She was worried about her fruit when it turned cold last night. She said the stove might go out, and the *jars* might break."

Mrs. Peters' husband began to laugh. "Well, how about that for a woman! Held in *jail* for murder, and worrying about her jars of fruit!"

The attorney answered, "I guess before we finish with her, she may have something more important to worry about."

---

满了黏糊糊的东西。

　　"真恶心，"他生气地说。

　　"哦——她的水果，"彼得斯夫人说。她看了看黑尔夫人，又说："昨晚天气转冷，她就开始担心她的水果，说炉子一灭，坛子就得冻破。"

　　话音未落，她的丈夫就笑了起来。"哎，女人哪！都涉嫌谋杀进监狱了，还担心她那几坛子水果！"

　　律师应和说："我猜在结案之前，可能还有更重要的事情要她担心呢。"

---

sticky *adj.* 黏的；黏性的
jar *n.* （玻璃、陶瓷等制的）罐子

mess *n.* 混乱
jail *n.* 监狱

"Oh, well," Mr. Hale said, "women are used to worrying about nothing."

"And yet," said the attorney, "what would we do without the ladies?" He smiled at the women, but they did not speak, did not smile back.

The lawyer washed his hands and dried them on the *dishtowel*.

"Dirty towels!" he said. "Not much of a *housekeeper*, eh, ladies?" He kicked some *messy* pans under the *sink*.

"There's a lot of work to do around a farm," Mrs. Hale said

---

"哦，是啊，"黑尔先生说："女人嘛，就好没事瞎操心。"

"但是，"律师说："要是没有女人，我们可怎么办？"他冲在场的两个女人笑了笑，但没得到什么回应。

律师洗了洗手，又用抹布擦干。

"这些抹布可真脏！"他说。"这个主妇真不怎么样，对吧，女士们？"说完又踢了踢水槽下堆得乱糟糟的锅碗瓢盆。

"农场里的活那么多，"黑尔夫人厉声说："再说好多时候你们男人

---

dishtowel  *n.*  干毛巾布
messy  *adj.*  凌乱的

housekeeper  *n.*  家庭主妇
sink  *n.*  水槽

sharply. "And men's hands aren't always as clean as they might be."

"Ah! You feel a *duty* to your sex, I see!" He laughed. "But you and Mrs. Wright were neighbors. I guess you were friends, too."

"I've not seen much of her these years."

"And why was that? You didn't like her?"

"I liked her well enough. Farmers' wives have their hands full, Mr. Henderson. And then—it never seemed like a very happy place..."

"You mean the Wrights didn't *get on* very well together?"

"No. I don't mean anything. But I don't think a place would be happier if John Wright was in it."

"I'd like to talk to you more about that, Mrs. Hale. But first we'll

---

的手可不总是那么干净的。"

"呵呵，你觉得有义务替你们女人说话，我明白！"他笑着说："但是你从前和赖特夫人是邻居，我猜你们也是朋友吧。"

"我这些年很少见到她。"

"那是为什么？你不喜欢她吗？"

"我还是挺喜欢她的。可你哪知道农夫的妻子每天会有多忙，亨得森先生。而且，这个地方一直就不讨人喜欢……"

"你的意思是赖特夫妻关系不是很融洽？"

"不，我可没别的意思。但觉得约翰·赖特不管在哪儿都不会让人感到快乐。"

"我们以后再好好聊聊这事，黑尔太太。现在得先上楼看看了。"

---

duty *n.* 责任

get on 相处；进展

look upstairs."

The sheriff said to the attorney, "I suppose anything Mrs. Peters does will be all right? She came to take Mrs. Wright some clothes— and a few little things."

"Of course," said the attorney. "Mrs. Peters is one of us. Maybe you women may come on a *clue* to the *motive*—and that's the thing we need."

Mr. Hale smiled, ready to make a joke. "Yes, but would the women know a clue if they did come upon it?"

III

The women stood silent while the men went upstairs. Then Mrs.

---

警长对律师说："我太太在这儿做什么都行吧？她来替赖特夫人取些衣物——还有一些别的小物件儿。"

"当然没问题，"律师说："彼得斯夫人是和我们一起来的嘛。可能你们的夫人会找到一些有关作案动机的线索——那可正是我们所需要的。"

黑尔先生笑了，想开个玩笑："是啊，可是，就算一下子碰上了，她们知道那是线索吗？"

III

男人们上楼时，两个女人默默地站着。之后，黑尔夫人开始清理水槽

---

clue *n.* 线索                                    motive *n.* 动机；目的

Hale began to clean the messy pans under the sink.

"I would *hate* to have men coming into my kitchen, looking around and talking about my *housework*."

"Of course, it's their duty," Mrs. Peters said. But Mrs. Hale was looking around the kitchen herself. She saw a box of *sugar*. Next to it was a paper bag—half full.

"She was putting this in there," she said to herself. Work begun and not finished? She saw the table—a dishtowel lay on it. One half of the table was clean. What had interrupted Minnie Foster?

"I must get her things from the cupboard," Mrs. Peters said.

Together they found the few clothes Mrs. Wright had asked for.

---

下那一堆乱糟糟的锅碗瓢盆。

"我讨厌男人进我的厨房，东瞅西看，对家务活评头品足。"

"可不是吗，他们就是干这个的。"彼得斯夫人说。而黑尔夫人此刻正亲自在厨房巡视。她看见一个糖罐，旁边还有个纸袋——半空的。

"她当时正往糖罐里装糖呢，"她自言自语道。都装一半了，怎么没装完？她又看了看桌子——上面有一块抹布，桌子只擦净了一半。是什么让明妮·福斯特停下了手里的活儿？

"我得从柜子里给她拿些东西，"彼得斯夫人说。

她们俩一起找出赖特夫人想要的那几件衣服。黑尔夫人拿起了一件黑

---

hate *v.* 讨厌；憎恨          housework *n.* 家务事
sugar *n.* 糖

Mrs. Hale *picked up* an old black skirt.

"My, John Wright hated to spend money!" she said. "She used to wear pretty clothes and sing in the *church*, when she was Minnie Foster..." Martha Hale looked at Mrs. Peters and thought: she doesn't *care* that Minnie Foster had pretty clothes when she was a girl. But then she looked at Mrs. Peters again, and she wasn't sure. In fact, she had never been sure of Mrs. Peters. She seemed so nervous, but her eyes looked as if they could see a long way into things.

"Is this all you want to take to the jail?" Martha Hale asked.

"No, she wanted an apron and her *woolen* shawl." Mrs. Peters

---

色的旧裙子。

"天啊，约翰·赖特这么抠门！"她说："她以前可不是这样，朝气勃勃，穿着漂亮的衣服，在教堂里唱歌，那个时候她还叫明妮·福斯特……"玛撒·黑尔看着彼得斯夫人，心想：她才不会在乎明妮·福斯特嫁人前有没有漂亮衣服呢。但是，当她再次看着彼得斯夫人的时候，心里又有些拿不准了。事实上，对这个彼得斯夫人，她从来就琢磨不透。彼得斯夫人表情虽然显得紧张，但那双眼睛却好像能洞穿一切似的。

"这些东西你都要拿到监狱里去吗？"黑尔夫人问道。

"不，她只想要围裙和羊毛披肩。"彼得斯夫人边说边把这两样东西

---

pick up 捡起；拾起  
care v. 在乎

church n. 教堂  
woolen adj. 羊毛的

took them from the cupboard.

"Mrs. Peters!" cried Mrs. Hale suddenly. "Do you think she did it?"

Mrs. Peters looked frightened. "Oh, I don't know," she said.

"Well, I don't think she did," Mrs. Hale said. "Asking for her apron and her shawl. Worrying about her fruit."

"Mr. Peters says it looks bad for her," Mrs. Peters answered. "Saying she didn't wake up when someone *tied* that rope around his neck. Mr. Henderson said that what this *case* needs is a motive. Something to show anger—or sudden feeling."

"Well, I think it's kind of low to lock her up in jail, and then come out here to look for clues in her own house," said Martha Hale.

---

从柜子里拿了出来。

"彼得斯太太！"黑尔夫人突然喊道："你觉得是她干的吗？"

彼得斯夫人看起来很害怕，说："哦，我不知道，"

"嗯，我看不是她，"黑尔夫人说："不然，她怎么还会要围裙和披肩呢？还担心那些水果。"

"彼得斯先生说情况对她不利，"彼得斯夫人答道："有人把绳子勒在她丈夫的脖子上她竟然说她没醒。亨得森先生说这案子只缺一个作案动机，就是能够激起愤怒，或是激发情绪的事。"

"哼，我觉得这有点说不过去。先把她关进牢里，然后，到她房里东翻西找查线索，"玛撒·黑尔说。

---

tie *v.* 系　　　　　　　　　　　　　　　　　　　case *n.* 案件

"But, Mrs. Hale," said the sheriff's wife, "the law is the law."

Mrs. Hale turned to re-light the stove. "How would you like to cook on this broken thing year after year—?"

Mrs. Peters looked from the broken stove to the *bucket* of water on the sink. Water had to be carried in from outside. "I know. A person gets so down—and *loses heart*."

And again Mrs. Peters' eyes had that look of seeing into things, of seeing through things.

"Oh, look, Mrs. Hale. She was *sewing* a *quilt*." Mrs. Peters picked up a sewing basket full of quilt blocks.

The women were studying the quilt as the men came downstairs. Just as the door opened, Mrs. Hale was saying, "Do you think she

---

"但是，黑尔太太，"警长夫人说："法律就是法律。"

黑尔夫人转过身来，把炉火重新点燃。"在这种破炉子上做饭，年复一年，谁受得了——？"

彼得斯夫人看了看破旧的火炉，又看了看水槽上的那桶水（水要从外边提进来）。"我知道，一个人要是太压抑了，就会绝望的。"

彼得斯夫人眼里又一次出现了那种眼神，那种洞穿一切的眼神。

"啊，瞧，黑尔太太。她正在做被子呢。"彼得斯夫人拣起一个针线筐，里面装满了布片。

两个女人还在琢磨被子的事，几个男人下了楼。他们开门的时候，黑尔夫人正说："你觉得她是要把那些布片缝起来还是编起来？"

---

bucket *n.* 桶；水桶　　　　lose heart 失去信心
sew *v.* 缝　　　　quilt *n.* 被子

was going to quilt it, or just *knot* it?"

"Quilt it or knot it!" laughed the sheriff. "They're worrying about a quilt!" The men went out to look in the barn.

Then Mrs. Peters said in a strange voice, "Why, look at this one." She held up a quilt block. "The sewing. All the rest were sewed so nice. But this one is so messy—"

Mrs. Hale took the quilt block. She pulled out the sewing and started to *replace* bad sewing with good.

"Oh, I don't think we ought to touch anything..." Mrs. Peters said helplessly.

"I'll just finish this end," said Mrs. Hale, quietly.

---

"是缝起来还是编起来！"警长哈哈大笑。"她们还在操心一床被子！"几个男人出去看谷仓了。

这时，彼得斯夫人用一种奇怪的声音说道："哎呀，你看这个。"她举起了一块布片。"看这做工，别的都连得好好的，就这块连得一团糟——"

黑尔夫人拿起布片，把没连好的地方扯下来，重新连好。

"唔，我觉得我们不该碰这些东西……"彼得斯夫人无助地说。

"我马上就完，"黑尔夫人平静地说。

---

knot *v.* 把……打成结      replace *v.* 把……放回原处；替换

"Mrs. Hale?"

"Yes, Mrs. Peters?"

"What do you think she was so nervous about?"

"Oh, I don't know. I don't know that she was—nervous. Sometimes I sew badly when I'm tired."

She looked quickly at Mrs. Peters, but Mrs. Peters was looking far away. Later she said in an ordinary voice, "Here's a bird *cage*. Did she have a bird, Mrs. Hale? It seems kind of funny to think of a bird here. I wonder what happened to it."

"Oh, probably the cat got it."

"But look, the door has been *broken*. It looks as if someone was

---

"黑尔太太？"

"什么事儿，彼得斯太太？"

"你认为是什么事让她那么紧张？"

"嗯，我可真不知道，我甚至不知道她还紧张。有时候我也干不好，尤其是累了的时候。"

她很快地扫了彼得斯夫人一眼，可彼得斯夫人正目视远方。稍后，彼得斯夫人用平常的声音说："这有一个鸟笼。她养鸟吗，黑尔太太？在这想起一只鸟来好像有点好笑。不知道那鸟出了什么事。"

"嗯，可能是叫猫给吃了。"

"但是你看，笼子的门坏了，好像有人发狠弄坏的。"

---

cage  n. 笼　　　　　　　　　　　　　　　broken  adj. 损坏的

rough with it."

Their eyes met, worrying and *wondering*.

"I'm glad you came with me, Mrs. Hale. It would be lonely for me—sitting here alone."

"I wish I had come over here sometimes when she was here," answered Mrs. Hale. "I stayed away because it wasn't a happy place. Did you know John Wright, Mrs. Peters?"

"Not really. They say he was a good man."

"Well—good," Mrs. Hale said. "He didn't drink, and paid his *bills*. But he was a hard man. His voice was like the north wind that cuts

两人四目相对，满心焦虑和疑惑。

"你能和我一起来，我很高兴，黑尔太太。要是就我一个人坐在这里，肯定太孤独了。"

"没出事的时候，我要是能多来几趟就好了，"黑尔夫人答道："我不过来，是因为这儿真不是个让人高兴的地方。彼得斯太太，你认识约翰·赖特吗？"

"算不上认识，都说他是个好人。"

"嗯——倒是挺好，"黑尔夫人说："他不喝酒、不欠账。但也挺冷酷，他的声音就像刺骨的北风，让你不寒而栗。你不认识——她，对吧，

wonder *v.* 想知道

bill *n.* 账单；账款

to the bone. You didn't know—her, did you, Mrs. Peters?"

"Not until they brought her to the jail yesterday."

"She was—she was like a little bird herself... Why don't you take the quilt blocks in to her? It might take up her mind."

"That's a nice idea, Mrs. Hale," agreed the sheriff's wife. She took more quilt blocks and a small box out of the sewing basket.

"What a *pretty* box," Mrs. Hale said. "That must be something she had from a long time ago, when she was a girl." Mrs. Hale opened the box. Quickly her hand went to her nose.

Mrs. Peters *bent* closer. "It's the bird," she said softly. "Someone

---

彼得斯太太？"

　　"昨天他们把她带到牢里，我才认识。"

　　"她以前啊，简直就像一只小鸟……你为什么不把这些布片给她带去呢？好让她有点事干。"

　　"好主意，黑尔太太，"警长夫人表示赞同。从针线筐里又拿起一些布片，还有一个小盒子。

　　"多漂亮的小盒子啊，"黑尔夫人说："这应该是她很久以前的东西了，肯定是嫁人以前的。"黑尔夫人打开盒子，立刻用手捂住了鼻子。

　　彼得斯夫人俯身细看。"是那只鸟，"她轻轻地说："被人扭断了脖子。"

---

pretty *adj.* 漂亮的　　　　　　　　　bend *v.* （身体或头部）斜，偏向

broke its neck."

Just then the men came in the door. Mrs. Hale *slipped* the box under the quilt blocks.

"Well, ladies," said the county attorney, "have you *decided* if she was going to quilt it or knot it?" He smiled at them.

"We think," began the sheriff's wife nervously, "that she was going to—knot it."

"That's interesting, I'm sure," he said, not listening. "Well, there's no *sign* that someone came in from the outside. And it was their own rope. Now let's go upstairs again..." The men left the kitchen again.

---

正在这时，几个男人进了门。黑尔夫人赶紧把那个盒子塞到布片下面。

"好了，女士们，"郡律师面带微笑，说："你们确没确定她到底是要缝还是要编啊？"

"我们觉得，"警长夫人紧张地说："她是要——编。"

"真有意思，真的，"他嘴里这么说，耳朵却什么也没听进去。"好了，没有什么迹象表明凶手是从外边进来的，绳子也是他们自家的。我们还得再上楼看看……"男人们又离开了厨房。

---

slip *v.* 将某物放在某处（常指悄悄地）　　decide *v.* 决定
sign *n.* 迹象

"She was going to *bury* the bird in that pretty box," said Mrs. Hale.

"When I was a girl," said Mrs. Peters softly, "my *kitten*— there was a boy who murdered it, in front of my eyes. If they hadn't held me back, I would have—hurt him."

They sat without speaking or moving.

"Wright wouldn't like the bird. A thing that sang. She used to sing. He killed that, too," Mrs. Hale said slowly.

"Of course, we don't know who killed the bird," said Mrs. Peters.

"I knew John Wright," Mrs. Hale answered. "There had been

---

"她想用这个漂亮盒子把鸟埋了，"黑尔夫人说。

"我小时侯，"彼得斯夫人轻轻地说，"养过一只小猫——有个男孩把它给弄死了，就当着我的面。要不是有人拦着，我一定——饶不了他。"

她们坐在那儿，一言不发，一动不动。

"赖特不喜欢这只鸟，这是个会唱歌的东西。她以前爱唱歌，但也被他给扼杀了，"黑尔夫人缓缓地说。

"当然了，我们不知道是谁弄死了那只鸟，"彼得斯夫人说。

"我了解约翰·赖特，"黑尔夫人答道。"多少年了，她什么也没

---

bury *v.* 埋葬                                          kitten *n.* 小猫

years and years of—nothing. Then she had a bird to sing to her. It would be so—silent—when it stopped."

"I know what silence is," Mrs. Peters said in a strange voice. "When my first baby died, after two years..."

"Oh, I wish I'd come over here sometimes. That was a *crime*!" Mrs. Hale cried.

But the men were coming back. "No, Peters, it's all clear. *Except* the *reason* for doing it. If there was some real clue... Something to show the jury... You go back to town, sheriff. I'll stay and look around some more."

Mrs. Hale looked at Mrs. Peters. Mrs. Peters was looking at her.

---

有。后来就弄了一只鸟给她唱歌。要是鸟不唱了，这里会是一片死寂。"

"我可知道那滋味儿，"彼得斯夫人用一种奇怪的声音说："我第一个孩子死后，有两年呢……"

"唉，我要是能多来几次就好了。真是罪过啊！"黑尔夫人大声说。

男人们又回来了。"不，彼得斯，除了作案动机，别的都清楚了。要是能有一条真正的线索……，要是能有什么东西给陪审团看……你先回城，警长。我留下，再好好查看查看。"

黑尔夫人看看彼得斯夫人，彼得斯夫人也正看着她。

---

crime *n.* 罪；罪行          except *prep.* 除了
reason *n.* 理由；原因

"Do you want to see what Mrs. Peters is bringing to the jail?" the sheriff asked the attorney.

"Oh, I guess the ladies haven't picked up anything very dangerous," he answered. "After all, a sheriff's wife is *married* to the law. Did you ever think of your duty that way, Mrs. Peters?"

"Not—just that way," said Mrs. Peters *quietly*.

The men went out to get the buggy, and the women were alone for one last moment.

Mrs. Hale pointed to the sewing basket. In it was the thing that would keep another woman in jail.

---

"你想看看彼得斯夫人要往监狱里带什么东西吗？"警长问律师。

"啊，我猜女士们不会挑什么危险的东西，"律师答道："毕竟，嫁给警长就是嫁给了法律嘛。你是不是也这样看待你的职责啊，彼得斯太太？"

"并不完全是那样，"彼得斯夫人平静地说。

男人们出去准备马车，这是最后一次剩下两个女人单独在一起了。

黑尔夫人指了指针线筐，这里有个东西会让另一个女人坐牢。

一时间，彼得斯夫人没有动，但紧接着，她就跑过去拿那个小盒，使劲地往她的小手提包里塞，可是怎么也塞不进去。

---

married *adj.* 已婚的　　　　　　　　　　　　quietly *adv.* 安静地

For a moment Mrs. Peters did not move. Then she ran to get the box. She tried to put it in her little handbag, but it didn't fit.

There was the sound of the door opening. Martha Hale took the box and put it quickly in her big pocket.

"Well, Peters," said the county *attorney* jokingly, "at least we found out that she was not going to *quilt* it. She was going to—what do you call it, ladies?"

Mrs. Hale put her hand against her pocket. "We call it—*knot* it, Mr. Henderson."

---

这时传来了开门声。玛撒·黑尔接过盒子，利索地揣进了自己的大衣袋里。

"嗯，彼得斯，"郡律师开玩笑地说："至少我们知道她不是要缝被子，她是要——女士们，你们管那个叫什么来着？"

黑尔夫人用手护着衣袋，回答说："我们把它叫编，亨得森先生。"

---

attorney  *n.*  律师
knot  *v.*  把……打成结

quilt  *v.*  缝制（织物、被子）

# The Whale Hunt

Adapted from the novel *Moby Dick* by Herman Melville

Herman Melville was born in 1819 in New York City. In 1841, he went to sea again, this time on a whaling ship, the Acushnet. Melville spent four years on the whaling ship in the Pacific Ocean. His many *adventures* at sea formed the subject of several popular novels he wrote after returning from his *voyages*. The following story, "The Whale Hunt," is taken from his most famous novel, *Moby Dick*, *published* in 1851. The novel tells the adventures of a whaling ship, the Pequod, as it hunts Moby Dick, a huge

## 猎鲸

根据赫尔曼·麦尔维尔的小说《白鲸》改写

赫尔曼·麦尔维尔，1819年生于纽约市，1841年，他登上一艘捕鲸船出海捕鲸。他花了四年的时间在太平洋上捕鲸。多年的海上生涯为他日后若干小说的写作提供了素材。"猎鲸"选自其1851年出版的《白鲸》，小说讲述了在捕猎一条巨鲸时，捕鲸船"裴廊德号"上

adventure　*n.* 冒险　　　　　　　　　　　　voyage　*n.* 航海
publish　*v.* 出版

white sperm whale. *Moby Dick* is *considered* one of the greatest of all American novels, but it was not very popular when it was first published. During the last twenty-five years of his life, Melville worked as a customs inspector in New York City. He wrote poetry during these years, but his early popularity fell away. Just before his death in 1891, he completed another book about life at sea, *Billy Budd*, which brought him to public *attention* once more.

I

It was a hot, still afternoon. Storm clouds were *gathering* overhead. The whaling ship, Pequod, out of Nantucket, sailed smoothly across the lead-gray sea. The seamen were lazily lying on deck, or staring from the masts out to sea. All the men were still—still, too, the gray waters. Each silent *sailor* turned to his own dreaming.

---

发生的故事。如今《白鲸》被看作是美国最伟大的小说之一。但当它第一次出版时，并不是非常受欢迎。在麦尔维尔人生的最后二十五年，他的工作是海关检察员。在此期间，他从事了诗歌创作，但是他原来的声望有所下降。1891年，麦尔维尔告别人世。在此之前，他又写了另外一本关于海上生活的书《比利·巴德》，这部小说令他又一次声名鹊起。

I

正午过后，天气闷热，风平浪静。头顶乌云密布。捕鲸船"裴科德号"自南塔基特出航，平稳地驶向铅灰色的大海。水手们有的在甲板上懒洋洋横躺竖卧，有的在桅杆上凝望着海面。所有的人都默然不语，一如那寂静无声的铅灰色海面。每个沉默的水手都做起了自己的美梦。

---

consider  *v.* 认为；以为
gather  *v.* 聚集

attention  *n.* 注意力
sailor  *n.* 水手；海员

I, Ishmael, was one of that crew. I had signed onto the Pequod in Nantucket with Queequeg, a Polynesian *harpooner* of great strength and skill. We had become friends sailing with these men for many empty days, with no sight of a whale. We had worked with the men; we had eaten, sung, and shouted with them. Now Queequeg and I sat with the others on deck, our hands slowly working with *ropes* and *tools*, our minds lost in thought and silence.

Suddenly I awoke to a cry so strange, so wild, that the rope fell from my hand. I stood looking up at the dark clouds from which that voice had dropped like a wing. High up in the highest mast was our *lookout*, Tashtego, an Indian from Martha's Vineyard Island in Massachusetts. His body was reaching eagerly forward, his hand pointing straight ahead. His wild cry was the cry of whalemen all

---

　　我叫以赛玛利，是船上的水手，在南塔基特，我和一个叫魁魁格的人一起签约登船。这个来自波利尼西亚的捕鲸人，力大如牛，技艺高超。在跟这些船员一道航行的日日夜夜中，我们一无所获，连个鲸鱼的影子也没见到，但我们俩却成了朋友。我们跟那些人一同干活，一同吃饭，一同唱歌，一同喊叫。那天下午，魁魁格和我跟其他人一起坐在甲板上，我们这些人，有的手握绳索，有的手拿工具，都在懒洋洋地干活。大家都若有所思，沉默不语。

　　突然间我听到一声叫喊。那叫声非常奇特，非常狂野，吓得我连手里的绳子都掉下去。我站在那里仰望天上的乌云，那声音就像一只折断的翅膀从云端直冲而下。在最高的杆上高高站立着的是我们的瞭望员——来自马萨诸塞州的马撒葡萄园岛的塔斯蒂哥。他身体急切地前倾，一只手指向

---

harpooner　*n.* 鱼叉手

tool　*n.* 工具；用具

rope　*n.* 绳

lookout　*n.* 瞭望者

over the seas, from lookouts high up in the masts. But Tashtego's was the most *unearthly* and musical voice of all.

"There she blows! There! There! There! She blows! She blows!"

"Where—away?"

"There, to *leeward*, about two miles off! A school of them! Sperm whales, men!"

Instantly, everything was moving as we prepared for the hunt.

The sperm whale blows its jets of air and water as regularly as a clock ticks. This is how whalemen know them from other kinds of whale. The sperm whale is a clever, even *tricky* animal when it knows it is being hunted. But these whales had not seen us yet. Therefore the Pequod was now kept away from the wind, and she went gently

---

前方，叫声狂野，正是所有海域里捕鲸人从桅杆顶部高高的瞭望哨发出的叫喊。但塔斯蒂哥的声音最为奇特，也最为悦耳。

"她喷水了！在那儿！那儿！那儿！喷水了！喷水了！"

"在哪儿，多远？"

"在那儿，在下风处！大约两英里！有一群！是抹香鲸，伙计们！"

眨眼间，整条船都行动起来准备猎鲸了。

抹香鲸定时喷出气体和水柱，如同钟表一样准时，捕鲸人就凭这一点来识别它们。一旦知道自己成了猎杀的对象，抹香鲸就表现得很聪明，甚至很狡猾。但是眼下这一群还没有发现我们。因此，裴科德号避开风向，悄悄地

---

unearthly *adj.* 怪异的；神秘的　　　　leeward *n.* 下风处
tricky *adj.* 狡猾的

rolling before it. We expected the whales to rise up in front of our bow.

The men not already on deck dropped down from the masts on ropes. The *tubs* that held ropes for the *harpoons* were set out on deck. The boat crews gathered by their boats. We swung the four boats from the deck of the Pequod out over the sea.

"All ready, Fedallah?" Captain Ahab cried to his harpooner, a dark, dangerous-looking man from the East Asian islands.

"Ready," was the half-hissed *reply*. Fedallah wore a black Chinese jacket; his white hair was *wrapped* round and round his head. He had the hard, silent, deadly look that ordinary people see only in fearful

绕到鲸群前面。我们希望鲸群浮出水面时，能正好出现在船头前方。

槌杆上的人都顺着绳子滑了下来；装捕鲸叉用绳的大盆也都端到甲板上了。要下船捕捉的人员都聚在各自的小船旁。我们把四艘小船从裴科德号的甲板上吊起来移到海面上方。

"准备好了吗，费达拉？"亚哈船长冲着他的鱼叉手喊道。这个面色黝黑，样子凶险的鱼叉手来自东亚群岛。

"准备好了，"回答的声音有些嘶哑。费达拉穿着一件中国式短褂，白头发在头上盘了一圈又一圈，他长着一副严厉而又冷漠的、毫无生气的面孔，那是普通人只有在噩梦中才能看到的面孔。

tub *n.* 盆；桶　　　　harpoon *n.* 鱼叉
reply *n.* 回答　　　　wrap *v.* 缠绕

dreams.

"Lower the boats, then, do you hear? Lower away!" Captain Ahab shouted to the boat crew *chiefs*. The four boats were quickly lowered. The eager crews acted with an unconscious daring that is unknown in other *professions*. They jumped goat-like from the high deck of the Pequod down into the boats rolling on the waves below.

Captain Ahab stood tall in the *stern* of his boat. "Spread yourselves widely, all boats," he called to Starbuck, Stubb and Flask, the other boat crew chiefs. "You, Flask, pull out more to leeward."

"Aye, aye, Sir," little Flask answered happily. He swung around the great oar that steered his boat. "Lay back on those oars!" he ordered his crew. "There! There again! There she blows right ahead,

---

"放下小船，听到没有？放下去！"亚哈船长冲着各个小船的头儿喊道。四艘小船很快就放下去了。心急的船员们马上行动起来，动作中透出的勇敢、果断连他们自己都没意识到，外行人就更是无从知晓了。他们从裴科德号高高的甲板上山羊般敏捷地一跃而下，跳到下面随着波涛摇曳的小船上。

亚哈船长高高立于船尾。"各船注意，大范围散开！"他高声命令另外几条小船上的头儿——斯达巴克、斯塔布和弗拉斯克。"你，弗拉斯克，再往下风处靠靠。"

"是，是，船长。"矮小的弗拉斯克兴冲冲地答道。他回转着导航的大桨。"你们那些桨往后划！"他命令手下。"出来了！出来了！又出来了！就在前边，喷水了，小伙子们！往后划！"

---

chief  *n.* 首领；头目　　　　　　　　profession *n.* 职业；专业
stern  *n.* 船尾；末端

boys! Lay back!"

Starbuck was chief of my boat. Like the other crew chiefs, he stood in the stern of the boat holding the steering *oar*. We faced him, our backs to the whales ahead. As we headed past Stubb's boat, we could hear him talking to his crew: "Pull, pull on those oars, my fine hearts! Pull, my children, pull, my little ones," he called in a voice that was strong and low, smooth and musical. "Why don't you break your *backbones*, my boys? Still asleep, are you? Pull, will you? pull, can't you? pull, won't you? That's the way you'll get your gold, my lovely fellows! Hurrah for the gold cup of sperm oil, my *heroes*! Yes, and easy, easy; don't be in a hurry—don't be in a hurry. Why don't you break your oars, you dogs! That's it—that's it; long and strong.

---

　　我所在的这艘小船归斯达巴克管。他像其他小船上的头儿一样，也站在船尾掌舵。我们面对着他，后背对着小船前方的鲸鱼。在我们与斯塔布的小船擦身而过时，我听到他跟手下讲："划啊，使劲儿，我的宝贝儿。使劲划啊，我的娃娃。"声音强劲而低沉，流畅而悦耳。"小伙子们哪，还没累断腰？小坏蛋们哪，还在睡懒觉？快点划啊；快点划啊；快点划啊，使劲划啊，金子随便拿！勇士搏激流，金杯装鲸油！对了，轻松又自在，不要急匆匆——不要急匆匆。小坏蛋们哪，还没累断腰？就是这样划，分毫也不差。甩开膀子鼓足劲。咬住东西，小恶棍们，看我的！"

---

oar *n.* 桨 　　　　　　　　　　　　　backbone *n.* 脊柱；脊背
hero *n.* 英雄

Bite on something, you *devils*! Here!" he said, pulling his knife from his belt, "every mother's son of you, pull out your knife, and put it between your teeth! That's it, my great hearts, my children, that's it! Now you're pulling like something! Now you are strong as that steel *blade*, my boys!" That is how Stubbs taught his men the religion of rowing. He would say the most terrifying things to his crew, his voice full of fun and *fury*. But the fury only added to the fun, and in the end they pulled at their oars for the joke of the thing.

Starbuck, too, pushed us onward toward the whales. He spoke in a low voice, almost a hissing *whisper*, so deep was his passion for the hunt. "Strong, boys, strong. There's tubs of sperm oil ahead, and

---

他一边说，一边把腰刀抽出来，"有种的，都把刀拔出来，用牙咬住。就是这样，我的心肝儿，我的宝贝，就是这样！这会儿划得挺像样！小伙子们，划得快又好，强劲像钢刀！"斯塔布就是这样向他的水手们传授"划船经"的。他总是给他们说些最恐怖的事情，声音滑稽有趣，却又狂放不羁。那狂放更让人觉得有趣。所以到了最后，大家都是越划越有劲儿，越划越觉得有趣儿。

斯达巴克也同样激励着我们前行追鲸。他的声音低沉，几乎是沙哑的耳语，其中蕴涵着他那深沉的猎鲸激情。"使劲划呀，小伙子们，大盆的

---

devil  *n.*  家伙；恶魔

fury  *n.*  狂怒；暴怒

blade  *n.*  刀片

whisper  *n.*  耳语；私语

that's what we came for! Pull, my boys—sperm oil's the game. This is our duty and our profit. Duty and profit, hand in hand—pull boys!" Duty and profit: this was Starbuck's *religion*.

Captain Ahab *steered* his boat ahead of the others. His crew of Manila seamen were as strong as steel and whalebone. In the bow of the boat stood Fedallah, his harpoon ready. In the stern, old Ahab stood ready at the steering oar, as he had done in a thousand boat-lowerings before. All at once, his arm rose into the air in an odd movement and then remained fixed. His five oarsmen stopped pulling. Boat and crew sat still on the sea. *Instantly*, the three other boats behind Ahab paused on their way. The whales had suddenly

鲸油在等着，我们要的就是这个！使劲划呀，小伙子们，鲸油就是我们的猎物。我们就是猎鲸汉，我们就是要多赚钱！猎鲸汉，好好干，同心协力多赚钱——孩子们，使劲儿划呀！"好好干，多赚钱——这就是斯达巴克的信仰。

亚哈船长驾着小船冲在最前面。他的那伙马尼拉水手简直就是健如钢铁，强似鲸骨。在船首站着的是费达拉，他已经鱼叉在握，跃跃欲试。在船尾，老亚哈船长站在那里掌舵，就跟以前千百次驾驶小船追逐鲸鱼时一样。突然间，他以一种古怪的动作把一只手臂伸向空中，定住不动了。他的五个桨手一下子停止了划船。船和船员们都静止于海上。紧随亚哈船长的其他三条小船也都停了下来。鲸鱼群已突然间平稳地潜入那茫茫的蓝色

religion *n.* 宗教；信仰  steer *v.* 驾驶；掌舵
instantly *adv.* 立即地；马上地

and smoothly lowered themselves deeper down into the blue. Only Ahab, closer to them, had seen their movement. For the moment, the huge whales had *disappeared*.

II

"Every man look out along his oar!" Starbuck called to us. "You, Queequeg, stand up!" Queequeg's heart and harpoon both were ready. He stood up tall in the bow, his eager eyes on the spot where the whales were last seen. Starbuck stood in the stern coolly balancing himself to the rolling boat. Silently, *searchingly*, he eyed the wide blue eye of the sea.

Not very far away from us, Flask's boat lay *breathlessly* still. Flask stood in the stern, on the narrow top of a strong, thick post used to

---

之中。只有离他们较近的亚哈船长看到了这一幕。一时间，巨大的鲸群消失了。

II

"每个人都要盯住自己船桨所指的方向！"斯达巴克冲着我们高喊。"你，魁魁格，站起来！"魁魁格手擎鱼叉，心里早有准备。他高高地立于船首，目光急切地盯着刚才鲸群消失的地方。斯达巴克则在船尾沉着地随着摇晃的小船稳住自己的身体，一声不响，面对蔚蓝色的大海，极目搜寻。

离我们不远的地方，弗拉斯克那艘小船屏息静气，一动不动。弗拉斯克站在船尾一根粗墩墩的圆柱上。当叉中的鲸游走的时侯，叉绳就是由这

---

disappear v. 消失；失踪      searchingly adv. 探究地；彻底地
breathlessly adv. 屏息地

guide the harpoon ropes when a harpooned whale pulls the boat along behind it. The post was short. Flask, too, was short—small and short. At the same time, he was big and tall in his *passion*. The post did not *satisfy* him.

"I can't see three waves off. Hold up an oar, there, and let me stand on that."

At his chief's word, Daggoo, Flask's huge African harpooner, moved to the stern. "I'm as good an oar as any, Sir," he said. "Will you *climb up*?"

With that, Daggoo planted his feet against the sides of the boat. He held out his hands to help Flask climb. Flask jumped up high and dry on Daggoo's shoulders.

---

根圆柱导出去的。圆柱很短，弗拉斯克也不高，可以说又矮又小。然而，此时他却人小热情高，这根柱子满足不了他。

"三个浪以外就看不清了。把桨举起来，我踩上去看看。"

弗拉斯克手下那个高大的非洲裔鱼叉手达谷听到命令后走向船尾。"什么桨能比我的肩膀管用，头儿？"他说，"上来吧。"

说完，达谷双脚靠船帮站稳，又伸出双手扶着弗拉斯克往上爬。弗拉斯克跳上去，高高跃起，镇定地站到了达谷的肩上。

---

passion *n.* 激情；热情
climb up 爬上去

satisfy *v.* 满足

"Thank you very much, my fine fellow," said Flask. "Only, I wish you fifty feet taller!"

At any time it is a strange sight to see the wonderfully *unconscious* ability of the whaleman. He can stand balanced in his boat even when the seas are rolling and crashing furiously under his feet. But to see the little Flask atop the tall Daggoo was even stranger. The black man rolled with every roll of the sea, and with the cool, easy, unthinking *command* of a king. And though chief of the boat, Flask balanced like a snow-flake on Daggoo's broad back. Now and then, Flask would shout, or stamp his foot on Daggoo's shoulder in his *eagerness* to find the whales. But Daggoo never moved, except with

---

"太谢谢了，我的好伙计，"弗拉斯克说。"你要是有50英尺高就好了！"

任何时候看到捕鲸人拥有这种奇妙的不自觉的本领都是一副奇观：他们能够稳立船头，任脚下惊涛骇浪，汹涌澎湃。而看到矮小的弗拉斯克站在高大的达谷肩上，就更让人称奇了。波涛汹涌，黑人随之起伏，他肩上的"国王"冷静、从容、不假思索地发出指令。弗拉斯克，小船上的头儿，在达谷宽阔的肩背上摇摆着保持平衡，有如风中飘飞的雪片。因为急于寻找鲸群，他在达谷的肩上时而叫喊，时而跺脚。达谷呢，他一动

---

unconscious *adj.* 无意识的　　　　command *n.* 指挥；命令
eagerness *n.* 渴望；热心

the roll of the sea. So it is with human wishes: We shout and stamp upon the forgiving earth in our passion, but the earth does not change her seas or seasons because of us.

Meanwhile, in the third boat, Stubb showed no such far-looking passion as Starbuck and Flask. The whales might be down for a short dive out of fear, or a longer dive to find food. In either case, Stubb would wait calmly with the aid of his *pipe*. He pulled it out of his hat-band, where he always wore it like a *feather*. But he hardly had time to light a match across the rough skin of his hand. Tashtego, Stubb's harpooner, stood with eyes *staring* to leeward like two fixed stars. Suddenly he dropped down to his seat.

---

不动，只是随着海浪在摇晃。人类的愿望就是这样：我们喊啊叫啊，性情所至踩着踏着宽广慈悲的地球，可地球呢，她从不因为我们而改变她的海水、她的季节。

这期间，在第三艘小船上，斯塔布可不像斯达巴克和弗拉斯克那样热心地远眺。鲸群可能只是出于恐惧，短期下潜。下潜的时间也可能会长些，那不过是在寻找食物。不论是哪一种情况，斯塔布都会点上烟斗，耐心等待。他总是把烟斗像一根羽毛一样别在帽檐上，这一次他刚刚取下烟斗，还没来得及在粗糙的手上划着一根火柴，他的鱼叉手塔斯蒂哥，两眼放着光盯着下风处某地，然后突然一屁股跌回到自己的座位上。

---

pipe  *n.*  烟斗                     feather *n.* 羽毛
stare  *v.* 凝视；盯着看

"Down, down all, and pull!—There they are!" he cried.

No landsman would have sensed the nearness of the whales at that moment. Nothing showed but a troubled bit of *greenish* water. A thin white fog blew past the waves to leeward. The air around seemed to move, like the air over heated plates of steel. And beneath this troubled pool of air and sea the whales moved onward, faster, faster than the boats could row.

"Pull, pull, my good boys," Starbuck called to us in his low-hissed, *passionate* whisper. He did not say much to his crew, nor did we say much to him. But the silence of the boat was sometimes broken by his strange whispers, now sharp with command, now *soft* with begging.

---

"快坐下，都坐下，快点划！——鲸群在那儿！"他喊道。

没有出过海的人根本感受不到那一刻鲸鱼的迫近。除了略微呈现绿色的海水以外，什么也看不出来。一层薄薄的白雾掠过海浪向下风处飘去。周围的空气也骚动起来，如同烧热的钢板上方那蒸腾的热气。在这翻腾的一方空气和海水的下方，鲸群正向前移动，越来越快，越来越快，比我们的船划得还快。

"弟兄们，划呀，划呀，"斯达巴克语调低沉，声音嘶哑，饱含激情。他不跟我们多说，我们也不跟他多说。船上的沉默气氛偶尔会被他低沉的嗓音打破，一会儿是厉声命令，一会儿是软语恳求。

---

greenish  *adj.* 呈绿色的                    passionate  *adj.* 热情的
soft  *adj.* 柔软的；温和的

How different from Starbuck was Flask!"Sing out and roar, my good hearts! Row our boat to the whale's broad back! On, on! Pull, pull!—only get me there, and I will give you my house, my wife, my children. Row on! I will go mad! Look at that white water!" Flask pulled his hat from his head, *stamped* up and down on it, picked it up, and finally threw it into the rolling sea.

"Look at that fellow now," said Stubb *philosophically* to his own crew. "He's all in a fury! But you, boys, pull smoothly onwards. Happily, happily-sweet *pudding* for supper, happy's the word. But pull softly-smooth, now—on those oars. Crack your backbones and bite your knives in two! Take it easy, I say, but break your heart and bones!"

---

　　弗拉斯克可就完全不同了！"唱起来，喊起来，弟兄们！把船划到鲸鱼背上去！划啊，快点！只要你们把我弄到那儿，你们要什么我就给什么，我的房子，我的老婆、孩子，随你们要！往前划！我都要疯了，看那白水啊！"弗拉斯克把头上的帽子扯下来，用脚跺着，接着又捡起来，最后扔到汹涌的海面上去了。

　　"看那家伙，"斯塔布像个哲学家似的对他的水手说。"他一见到鲸鱼就发狂。让他好好痛快痛快吧。不过，小伙子们，你们可要稳稳地向前划。要高兴点！高兴点！晚饭有甜布丁。就是要高兴。要划得柔，要划得稳。划吧，不停地划。咬碎钢刀划断脊梁骨！别紧张，我说，别着急，但要使尽全身的力！"

---

stamp *v.* 跺脚　　　　　　　　　philosophically *adv.* 哲学地
pudding *n.* 布丁

But what Captain Ahab said to his crew—those words should not be written here. Only the sharks in the terrific sea should give ear to his *furious* words, or see his eyes full of red murder. So did Ahab race to the hunt.

III

The chase was a scene full of quick wonder. The huge waves of the *all-powerful* sea rolled and roared. The men would take a deep breath as their boat balanced atop a wave sharp enough to cut it in two. Then they would slide down the other side, the harpooners and crew chiefs shouting, the oarsmen struggling. Then the long hard row up the opposite hill and the terrifying slide again down its other side. And behind the boats the wonderful sight of the Pequod

---

　　然而，亚哈船长对他的水手说的话，在这儿可是不该写出来的。可能只有令人恐怖的海洋里的鲨鱼才能倾听他那些狂怒的话，或是看到他那血红的嗜杀的双眼。亚哈穷追猎鲸时就是这副样子。

　　III

　　追逐猎鲸这一幕，充满奇观，瞬息万变。无所不能的大海掀起巨浪，翻腾咆哮。有时小船一跃而上那足以把它劈成两半的波峰，竭力保持平衡，水手们这时会倒吸一口冷气。越过波峰，小船就滑向浪底。鱼叉手和头儿们喊声连天，桨手们拼命划船。接着小船又艰难地跃上另一个波峰，然后又惊险地跌入浪底。裴科德号鼓足风帆，紧随小船，这奇妙的一幕，

---

furious *adj.* 激烈的；狂怒的　　　　　　all-powerful *adj.* 全能的

following fast, her sails wide to the wind. All this filled, and over-filled, the men's hearts. No one can feel stranger or stronger passion than one who for the first time enters the furious circle of the hunted sperm whale.

The dancing white water over the whales was becoming more visible as the clouds darkened. The *jets* of water and air coming from the whales began to spread out right and left as the whales separated from each other. Our boats pulled further apart, following them.

On Starbuck's boat, we had put up our *sail*. We rushed forward so fast in the rising wind that the leeward oars were almost torn from our hands. As the storm gathered, fog blew down over the waves.

---

让所有的水手壮志满腔，兴奋不已。没有什么比得上第一次加入猎杀抹香鲸的狂暴战团更让人感觉奇特，激情满怀了。

黑云低垂，衬得鲸鱼上方翻腾的白水更加清晰。鲸群开始四散逃命，喷出的水柱也就东倒西歪。我们的小船则开始分头追击鲸鱼。

在斯达巴克的船上，我们扬起了风帆。风越刮越猛，船越开越快，向下风划的时候，船桨几乎要脱手而去。风暴聚集，浓雾低垂，笼罩在波涛

---

jet n. 喷射流                                           sail n. 帆；风帆

Soon we were running through a thick cloud of it and could see neither the big ship Pequod nor any of the other small boats.

"There's white water again, men," Starbuck whispered. "There's time yet to kill a whale before the storm breaks. Stand up, Queequeg!" Queequeg, harpoon in his hand, stood tall. "There's his back," said Starbuck. "There, there, give it to him!"

A short, hissing sound leapt out of the boat; it was the pointed steel of Queequeg's harpoon. Then, all in a *terrific* movement, an unseen push came up under the stern. The *bow* of the boat seemed to *strike* a hill. Something rolled and thundered beneath us just as the storm broke overhead. The sail blew apart into pieces. The boat turned, and we were thrown, breathless, into the furious white

之上。很快我们就迷失于一片浓云迷雾之中，裴科德号和其他小船都看不见了。

"看，那边又有白水了。"斯达巴克低声说。"风暴要来了，但我们还来得及捕猎一条鲸鱼。魁魁格，站起来！"魁魁格手拿猎鲸叉，高高地站立着。"瞧，那是鲸背，"斯达巴克说，"在那儿，在那儿，瞄准了给他一家伙！"

只听"嗖"的一声，魁魁格手中锋利的猎鲸叉飞了出去。紧接着，我们的船尾就被一种看不见的力极为凶猛地推了一下，船头好像撞到了一座小山。船下有什么东西在奔涌咆哮，一如头上隆隆的风暴。风帆撕成了碎片，船翻了，我们被抛进惊涛骇浪之中，无法喘息。风暴、鲸鱼、猎鲸叉

terrific *adj.* 很大的；巨大的　　　　　　　　　　bow *n.* 船首
strike *v.* 撞击

waves. Storm, whale and harpoon had all mixed together. And the whale, only touched by the steel, *escaped*.

The boat was half filled with water but not broken. Swimming round it, we caught the floating oars, and pulled ourselves back into the boat. There we sat, up to our knees in sea, the water covering every bone and board.

Now the wind increased to a roar, and the waves crashed around the boat and into it. Thunder and lightning cracked around us. We shouted to the other boats, but our voices were *useless* in the rising storm. The fog hid the Pequod from us completely.

Starbuck struggled with the *waterproof matchbox*. After many failures he managed to light a tiny lamp. He handed it to Queequeg

---

统统乱作一团。那条鲸鱼，仅仅被钢叉碰了一下，马上逃走了。

小船里灌进一半水，好在没有断裂。我们在小船周围游着，捞起漂浮的船桨，然后爬回小船里。坐在船里，膝盖以下都没在海水中，那彻骨的冷水浸泡着我们的每一根骨头和船上的每一块木板。

海面上狂风大作，波涛汹涌。海浪冲击着小船，海水涌入舱内，四周电闪雷鸣。我们呼喊着其他几艘小船，但是声音很快就被风雷声和浪涛声淹没了。随着浓雾聚集，夜幕降临，裴科德号完全隐没不见了。

斯达巴克努力划着防水火柴，费了好大劲终于点着了一盏小小的灯笼。他把灯笼交给魁魁格，让他绑在了猎鲸叉顶端。然后，他坐下来，手

---

escape *v.* 逃脱　　　　　　　　　　　useless *adj.* 无用的；无效的
waterproof *adj.* 防水的　　　　　　　matchbox *n.* 火柴盒

to tie to the end of his harpoon. There, then, he sat, holding up that foolish candle in the heart of that terrible *emptiness*. There, then, he sat, through the dark hours of the night, hopelessly holding up hope in the middle of nothingness.

Wet to the bone, cold to the heart, we lifted our eyes as morning came on in the dark sky. Fog still lay spread out over the sea. The empty lamp lay broken at the bottom of the boat. Suddenly Queequeg jumped up, holding a hand to his ear. Through the lessening sounds of the storm, we could hear a *faint* sighing and cracking of ropes and masts in the wind.

The sound came nearer and nearer, until the fog was broken by a huge, *ghostly* form. Terrified, we jumped into the sea as the Pequod

里举着那缕微不足道的烛光，心中是一片可怕的空虚。他就坐在那里，透过漫漫长夜，在虚无之中绝望地举着获救的希望。

这一夜真是寒湿入骨，冷彻肺腑。漆黑的夜空终于露出了曙光，我们举目观望，海面上依然浓雾弥漫。那盏灯早已掉在船底，破碎了。突然，魁魁格跳了起来，一只手附在耳边倾听。通过正在减弱的风暴声，可以隐约听到风吹桅杆和缆绳发出的声音。

声音越来越近，直到一个庞然大物冲破迷雾。大家都吓得纷纷跳入海

emptiness *n.* 空虚　　　　　　　　　faint *adj.* 虚弱的；模糊的
ghostly *adj.* 可怕的；幽灵的

rose up behind and above us, only a ship's length away. Floating on the waves, we watched as our empty boat was pulled under the Pequod's bow, like a wood chip in a *waterfall*. Then it was gone. We swam hard for the Pequod. We were thrown against its side by the crashing waves, but at last were taken up and safely landed on *deck*.

And what of the other whale boats? Before the storm closed in, the other crews had cut lose from their whales and returned to the Pequod in good time. They all believed that our crew was lost under the furious waves. But still they sailed *nearby*, thinking to find a sign of our passing—a lonely oar, perhaps, floating on the endless sea.

---

里，原来是裴科德号从后面压了过来，离我们只有一个船身的距离。漂浮于波涛之上，我们眼看着空空的小船被裴科德号压入船首，如同瀑布中的一块小木屑一样，转眼就不见了。我们奋力游向裴科德号。汹涌的波浪把我们推到她的侧面，大伙终被救起，平安地登上了大船。

那么，其他几艘小船的命运如何呢？风暴到来之前，他们就不再追踪鲸群，及时返回了裴科德号。他们都认为在怒海狂涛之下，我们这一伙人肯定丧生了。但他们还是在附近转悠，希望能够找到我们的遗物，比方说一条孤零零的船桨，漂浮于浩瀚无边的大海之上。

---

waterfall *n.* 瀑布　　　　　　　　　　　　　　　　　deck *n.* 甲板
nearby *adv.* 在附近

# 03

# **P**aste

Adapted from the story by Henry James

**H**enry James was born in 1843 in Washington Place, New York. His father was a well-known *religious* thinker; his older brother, William James, became a famous *philosopher*. James was educated in New York and Europe and attended Harvard Law School. His years of school in London, Paris, and Geneva gave him a love for Europe. He traveled often to Europe, and after 1876 he made his home in London. James wrote widely. In addition to plays, *criticism*, and short stories, he wrote about twenty novels. *The Europeans*, *Washington Square*, *The Portrait of a Lady*, and *The*

# 真假珍珠

根据亨利·詹姆斯的同名故事改写

**亨**利·詹姆斯1843年生于纽约。他的父亲是一位著名的宗教思想家。他的哥哥——威廉·詹姆斯是一位著名的哲学家。他是在美国和欧洲受的教育，伦敦、巴黎和日内瓦的求学经历使他对欧洲产生了深厚的感情。他常去欧洲旅行，1876年开始定居伦敦。詹姆斯的写作题材广泛，除了戏剧、评论和短篇故事以外，还写了大约二十部小说，其中，最著名的作品包括《欧洲人》、《华盛顿广场》、《贵妇人画像》及

religious *adj.* 宗教的　　　　　　　　　　　philosopher *n.* 哲学家
criticism *n.* 评论；批评

# PASTE

*Bostonians* are among the best known. Much of James's work deals with the contrast in values and *behavior* of Americans and Europeans. He became a British citizen shortly before his death in 1916.

I

"I've found a lot more of her things," Charlotte's cousin said to her after his stepmother's *funeral*. "They're up in her room—but they're things I wish you'd look at."

Charlotte and her cousin, Arthur Prime, were waiting for lunch in the garden of Arthur's father, who had been a country *minister*. It seemed to Charlotte that Arthur's face showed the wish to *express* some kind of feeling. It was not surprising that Arthur should feel something. His stepmother had recently died, only three weeks after his father's death.

---

《波士顿人》。詹姆斯许多作品都涉及美国人和欧洲人在价值观和行为方面的差异。他1916年去世前不久加入英国国籍。

I

"我又发现了她的很多东西，"夏洛特的表兄在继母的葬礼结束后对她说。"都在楼上她房间里——我希望你能上去看看。"

夏洛特和表兄亚瑟·普拉姆正在亚瑟父亲的花园里等着吃午饭。亚瑟的父亲是一位乡村牧师。夏洛特觉得从亚瑟的表情上看，好像有什么感觉想要表达。亚瑟有什么感觉，这并不奇怪。他的继母刚刚去世，这是在父亲去世仅仅三周后。

---

behavior *n.* 行为；举止
minister *n.* 牧师

funeral *n.* 葬礼
express *v.* 表达

Charlotte had no money of her own and lived with a wealthy family as *governess* for their children. She had asked for leave to *attend* the funeral. During her stay Charlotte had noticed that her cousin seemed somehow to grieve without sorrow, to suffer without pain. It was Arthur's habit to drop a comment and leave her to pick it up without help. What "things" did he mean now? However, since she hoped for a *remembrance* of her stepaunt, she went to look at these "things" he had spoken of.

As she entered the darkened room, Charlotte's eyes were struck by the bright jewels that *glowed* on the table. Even before touching them, she guessed they were things of the theater. They were much too fine to have been things of a minister's wife. Her stepaunt had worn no jewelry to speak of, and these were crowns and necklaces,

---

　　夏洛特没有什么钱，她跟一户有钱人家生活在一起，当家庭教师。她这次去参加葬礼是事先请了假的。在表兄家逗留期间，夏洛特注意到表兄不知何故看起来忧而不悲，苦而不痛。亚瑟有个习惯，就是：丢下一句话，让她自己去琢磨。他说的"东西"是指什么呢？然而，既然她想纪念继舅妈，就不妨去看看他说的这些"东西"。

　　夏洛特走进那阴暗的房间，一眼就看到桌子上令人眼花缭乱的珠宝。还没有伸手去摸，就猜出这些东西都是演戏的道具。它们实在太精美了，不可能是一个牧师妻子的物品。继舅妈生前佩戴的东西根本谈不上是珠宝，而这些都是王冠、项链、钻石和金子。吃了一惊之后，夏洛特把它们

---

governess　*n.* 女家庭教师
remembrance　*n.* 纪念；追忆

attend　*v.* 出席；参加
glow　*v.* 绚丽夺目

diamonds and gold. After her first shock, Charlotte picked them up. They seemed like proof of the far-off, faded story of her stepaunt's life. Her uncle, a country minister, had lost his first wife. With a small son, Arthur, and a large *admiration* for the theater, he had developed an even larger admiration for an unknown actress. He had offered his hand in marriage. Still more surprisingly, the actress had accepted. Charlotte had *suspected* for years that her stepaunt's acting could not have brought her either *fame* or *fortune*.

"You see what it is—old stuff of the time she never liked to mention."

Charlotte jumped a little. Arthur must have followed her upstairs. He was watching her slightly nervous recognition of the jewelry.

---

捧在手上。它们看上去就像是对继舅妈那遥远的、依稀的故事的见证。舅舅是个乡村牧师。第一个妻子去世后，留给他一个小男孩，亚瑟。他对看戏十分着迷，对一个不知名的女演员更是鬼迷心窍，便向她求婚。更令人吃惊的是，那女演员居然接受了求婚。夏洛特疑惑了多年来，觉得继舅妈的做法既不会给自己带来名望，也不会带来财富。

"你明白这都是些什么了吧——都是些她从不愿提起的旧玩意儿。"

夏洛特惊跳起来。原来是亚瑟跟着她上楼来了。他在观察她见到这些珠宝后略微紧张的反应。

---

admiration *n.* 钦佩；赞赏　　　　suspect *v.* 怀疑；猜疑
fame *n.* 名声；名望　　　　fortune *n.* 财富

"I thought so myself," she replied. Then, to show intelligence without sounding silly, she said, "How *odd* they look!"

"They look awful," said Arthur Prime. "Cheap glass diamonds as big as potatoes. Actors have better taste now."

"Oh," said Charlotte, wanting to sound as *knowledgeable* as he, "now actresses have real diamonds."

"Some of them do."

"Oh, I mean even the bad ones—the *nobodies*, too."

Arthur *replied* coldly, "Some of the nobodies have the biggest jewels. But Mama wasn't that sort of actress."

---

"我也是这么想的，"她回答说。接着，为了表现出睿智，让人听起来不俗，她又说："它们看上去好古怪啊！"

"它们看上去很糟糕，"亚瑟·普拉姆说。"都是些廉价的玻璃钻石，个头大得像土豆。演员现在的口味可比以前高了。"

"哦，"夏洛特想要使自己的话听起来跟表兄一样有见识，就说，"现在演员都戴真钻石了。"

"有一些演员的确是这样。"

"哦，我是说就连糟糕的演员——还有无名小卒也是。"

亚瑟冷冷地回答说，"有些无名小卒佩戴最大的宝石。但妈妈可不是

---

odd *adj.* 古怪的；奇怪的　　　　　　knowledgeable *adj.* 有学识的
nobody *n.* 无名小卒；小人物　　　　　reply *v.* 回答；答复

"A nobody?" Charlotte asked.

"She wasn't a nobody that someone would give—well, not a nobody with diamonds. This stuff is *worthless*."

There was something about the old theater pieces that *attracted* Charlotte. She continued to turn them over in her hands.

Arthur paused, then he asked: "Do you care for them? I mean, as a remembrance?"

"Of you?" Charlotte said quickly.

"Of me? What do I have to do with it? Of your poor, dead aunt, who was so kind to you," he said *virtuously*.

---

那种演员。

"无名小卒？"夏洛特问。

"她不是那种无名小卒，要什么人给她送——呃，不是一个佩戴钻石的无名小卒。这些东西没有什么价值。"

这些旧道具里有着某种东西吸引着夏洛特。她继续在手里翻弄着。

亚瑟顿了顿，又问："你喜欢这些东西吗？我是说，作为纪念物？"

"算你送的？"夏洛特急切地说。

"我送的？我跟这个有什么关系？是你那可怜的、已故的舅妈，她对你那么好，"他很有良心地说。

---

worthless　*adj.* 无价值的；不值钱的　　　　　　　attract　*v.* 吸引
virtuously　*adv.* 善良地

"Well, I would rather have them than nothing."

"Then please take them." His face expressed more hope than *generosity*.

"Thank you." Charlotte lifted two or three pieces up and then set them down again. They were light, but so large and false that they made an *awkward* gift.

"Did you know she had kept them?"

"I don't believe she knew they were there, and I'm sure my father didn't. Her *connection* with the theater was over. These things were just put in a *corner* and forgotten."

Charlotte wondered, "What corner had she found to put them in?"

---

"哦，我倒宁愿有这些东西，总比一无所有强啊。"

"那你就拿去吧。"从他的表情上看，倒是更希望她赶快拿走，而不是出于慷慨大度。

"谢谢。"夏洛特拿起一两件，又放下了。它们的分量很轻，但个头大，一看就知道是赝品，作为礼品送人实在是太糟糕。

"你知道她一直都保留这些东西吗？"

"我想她根本不知道还有这些东西，我敢肯定父亲也不知道。她跟戏院已经没有关系了。这些东西不过是放在角落里，早被遗忘了。"

夏洛特很纳闷，"她找到了一个怎样的角落来放这些东西呢？"

---

generosity   *n.*  慷慨；大方          awkward   *adj.*  使人难堪的；令人尴尬的
connection   *n.*  联系；关联          corner   *n.*  角落

"She hadn't found it, she'd lost it," Arthur *insisted*. "The whole thing had passed from her mind after she put the stuff into a box in the schoolroom *cupboard*. The box had been stuck there for years."

"Are you sure they're not worth anything?" Charlotte asked *dreamily*.

But Arthur Prime had already asked himself this question and found the answer.

"If they had been worth anything, she would have sold them long ago. Unfortunately, my father and she were never wealthy enough to keep things of value locked up."

He looked at Charlotte for *agreement* and added, like one who is unfamiliar with generosity, "And if they're worth anything at all—why,

---

"她不是找到了，而是遗忘了，"亚瑟坚持说。"她把这些东西装进一个箱子里，放在教室的橱柜之后就把这一切都忘在了脑后。这个箱子原封未动，有好几年了。"

"你肯定这些东西一文不值吗？"夏洛特迷茫地问。

但亚瑟·普拉姆已经问过自己这个问题，而且已经找到了答案。

"这些东西真要是值什么钱的话，她早就给卖了。遗憾的是，我父亲和她从未富到把宝物锁起来的程度。"

他等着夏洛特表示赞许，接着，又像个不熟悉慷慨大度是怎么回事的人似的补充说，"假如它们还值点钱的话——那就更欢迎你拿去了。"

---

insist *v.* 坚持；强调
dreamily *adv.* 梦似地；恍惚地

cupboard *n.* 橱柜
agreement *n.* 同意；赞同

you're all the more welcome to them."

Charlotte picked up a small silk bag. As she opened it she answered him, "I shall like them. They're all I have."

"All you have—?"

"That *belonged to* her."

He looked around the poor room as if to question her *greed*. "Well, what else do you want?"

"Nothing. Thank you very much." As she said this she looked into the small silk bag. It held a necklace of large *pearls*.

"Perhaps this is worth something. Feel it." She passed him the necklace.

---

夏洛特拿起一个小丝袋，一边打开，一边回答说，"我会喜欢它们的。我只有这些东西。"

"你只有这些——？"

"那是属于她的。"

他四下看看这可怜巴巴的屋子，就好像是对她的贪婪表示疑问。"那么，你还想要什么？"

"什么都不要了。非常感谢你。"说着，她就朝小丝袋里面看。里面装的是一条大珍珠项链。

"这个东西也许能值一些钱。你摸摸。"她把项链递给他。

---

belong to 属于                    greed  *n.* 贪婪；贪心
pearl  *n.* 珍珠

He weighed it in his hands without interest. "Worthless, I'm sure—it's paste."

"But is it paste?"

He spoke *impatiently*. "Pearls nearly as large as nuts?"

"But they're heavy," Charlotte insisted.

"No heavier than anything else," he said, as if amused at her *simplicity*.

Charlotte studied them a little, feeling them, turning them around.

"Couldn't they possibly be real?"

"Of that size? Put away with that stuff?"

"Well, I *admit* it's not likely," Charlotte said. "And pearls are so

---

他在手里毫无兴趣地掂了掂。"不值钱，我敢肯定——这是假珍珠。"

"是假珍珠？"

他不耐烦地说："有像坚果那么大的珍珠吗？"

"不过，它们可是挺沉的，"夏洛特坚持说。

"也不比别的沉，"他说，好像对她的头脑简单感到好笑似的。

夏洛特又用手摸一摸，翻来倒去地研究了一会儿。

"不可能是真的吗？"

"就凭那个头吗？就凭跟那些东西扔在一起吗？"

"嗯，我承认不大可能是真的，"夏洛特说。"而且珍珠很容易仿制

---

impatiently *adv.* 不耐烦地          simplicity *n.* 简单

admit *v.* 承认

easily *imitated*."

"Pearls are not easily imitated, to anyone who knows about them. These have no shine. Anyway, how would she have got them?"

"Couldn't they have been a present?" Charlotte asked.

Arthur looked at her as if she had said something *improper*. "You mean because actresses are *approached* by men who—" He stopped suddenly. "No, they couldn't have been a present," he said sharply, and left the room.

Later, in the evening, they met to discuss Charlotte's *departure* the next day. At the end of the conversation, Arthur said,

"I really can't let you think that my stepmother was at any time of her life a woman who could—"

---

的。"

"对那些真正懂行的人来说，珍珠很不容易仿制的。这些东西没有光。不管怎么说，她怎么得到的呢？"

"不会是收到的礼物吗？"夏洛特问。

亚瑟看着她，就好像她说了什么不得体的话似的。"你是说男人想接近女演员，他们就——"他突然打住。接着又尖锐地说："不，它们绝对不可能是礼物。"说完，他就离开了房间。

后来，到了晚上，他们聚在一起商量夏洛特第二天要走的事。谈话要结束时，亚瑟说，

"我真的不能让你觉得继母在她一生中的任何时候是一个——"

---

imitate *v.* 仿效；模仿
approach *v.* 接近

improper *adj.* 不适当的；不合适的
departure *n.* 离开

"Accept expensive presents from admirers?" Charlotte added. Somehow Arthur always made her speak more directly than she meant to. But he only answered, seriously,

"Exactly."

"I didn't think of that, when I spoke this morning," said Charlotte *apologetically*, "but I see what you mean."

"I mean that her virtue was above question," said Arthur Prime.

"A hundred times yes."

"Therefore she could never have *afforded* such pearls on her small *salary*."

"Of course she couldn't," Charlotte answered *comfortingly*. "Anyway," she continued, "I noticed that the clasp that holds the

---

"接受崇拜者贵重礼物的女人？"夏洛特补充说。不知怎么搞的，亚瑟总能让她一开口就直言不讳，可她心里并不想这样。但他只回答了两个字：

"没错。"语气很严肃。

"我今天早晨说话的时候，并没有想到这一点，"夏洛特很抱歉地说，"现在才明白你的意思。"

"我的意思是她的品德根本不成问题，"亚瑟·普拉姆说。

"百分之百正确。"

"所以，她靠那么一点薪水根本就买不起珍珠项链。"

"当然买不起，"夏洛特安慰他说。"不管怎么说，"她又接着说，

---

apologetically  *adv.* 道歉地；认错地
salary  *n.* 薪水

afford  *v.* 买得起
comfortingly  *adv.* 安慰地

pearls together isn't even gold. I suppose it wouldn't be, with false pearls."

"The whole thing is cheap paste," Arthur announced, as if to end their *discussion*. "If the pearls were real, and she had hidden them all these years—"

"Yes?" asked Charlotte *curiously*.

"Well, I wouldn't know what to think!"

"Oh, I see," said Charlotte, and their conversation ended.

II

When she was back at work again, the false jewels seemed silly to Charlotte. She wasn't sure why she had taken them. She put them away under *a pile of* clothing, and there they might have stayed,

---

"我注意到项链的挂钩都不是金的。我想，应该是假珍珠，所以不用金的。"

"整个东西就是廉价的假珍珠，"亚瑟宣布说，就好像要结束这场讨论似的。"假如珍珠是真的，那么，她藏了这么多年——"

"那又怎么样？"夏洛特好奇地问。

"噢，我都不知道该怎么想了！"

"哦，我知道了，"夏洛特说。他们的谈话也就结束了。

II

当她又回去工作后，她觉得那些假宝石好像很无聊。她闹不清自己为什么要拿这些东西。她把它们放在一堆衣物底下，这个地方没有人动，但

---

discussion *n.* 讨论；谈论                        curiously *adv.* 好奇地

a pile of 一堆

except for the arrival of Mrs. Guy.

Mrs. Guy was a strange little woman with red hair and black dresses. She had the face of a baby, but took command like a *general*. She was a friend of the family Charlotte worked for. She had come to organize a week of parties to *celebrate* the 21st birthday of the family's oldest son. She happily accepted Charlotte's help with the *entertainments*.

"Tomorrow and Thursday are all right, but we need to plan something for Friday evening," she *announced* to Charlotte.

"What would you like to do?"

"Well, plays are my strong point, you know," said Mrs. Guy.

They discussed plays and looked at the hats and dresses they

---

盖伊夫人的到来改变了这种状态。

盖伊夫人是个很奇怪的小女人，她长着一头红发，着一身黑装。有一张娃娃脸，但下起命令来却像个将军。她是夏洛特雇主家的朋友。是专程来组织为期一周的宴会庆祝这家大儿子二十一岁生日的。她很高兴地接受夏洛特帮助她准备娱乐活动。

"明天和周四都没问题了，但我们得筹划一下周五晚上的活动，"她对夏洛特宣布说。

"你愿意干什么？"

"哦，演戏是我的强项，你知道，"盖伊夫人说。

她们就谈起戏剧来，还把要穿戴的衣帽等拿出来看看。

---

general *n.* 将军　　celebrate *v.* 庆祝
entertainment *n.* 娱乐活动　　announce *v.* 宣布；宣告

might wear.

"But we need something to *brighten* these up," Mrs. Guy decided. "These things are too dull. Haven't you got anything else?"

"Well, I do have a few things..." Charlotte admitted slowly. She went to find the jewels for Mrs. Guy. "Perhaps they're too bright, they're just glass and paste."

"Larger than life!" Mrs. Guy was *excited*. "They are just what we need. They'll give me great ideas!"

The next morning she came to find Charlotte in the schoolroom.

"I don't understand where you got these pieces," she said to Charlotte.

---

"我们得用什么东西来点缀一下才好，"盖伊夫人果断地说。"这些东西太平淡了。你还有别的什么东西吗？"

"噢，我还真有些东西……"夏洛特慢吞吞地承认说。然后，就去给盖伊夫人找宝石。"这些东西可能太耀眼了，都是些玻璃和假珍珠。"

"比真的还大！"盖伊夫人很激动。"这正是我们所需要的。这下可有好主意了！"

第二天早晨，她到教室来找夏洛特。

"我不明白你是从哪儿弄到的这些东西，"她对夏洛特说。

---

brighten  *v.* 使明亮；使更美丽          excited  *adj.* 激动的；兴奋的

"They belonged to my aunt, who died a few months ago. She was an actress for several years. They were part of her theatrical *equipment*."

"She left them to you?"

"No; my cousin, her *stepson*, who naturally has no use for them, gave them to me as a remembrance of her. She was a dear, kind person, always so nice to me, and I was very fond of her."

Mrs. Guy listened with interest. "But it must be your cousin who is a 'dear, kind person.' Is he also 'always so nice' to you?"

"What do you mean?" asked Charlotte.

"Can't you guess?"

---

"这都是我舅妈的，她几个月前去世了。当过几年演员。这些东西是她的一部分道具。"

"她把这些东西留给你了？"

"不是。是我表兄，就是她的继子，他要这些东西没用，就把这些东西作为纪念物送给我了。她是一个非常可亲可爱的人，待我总是那么和蔼，我也非常喜欢她。"

盖伊夫人饶有兴趣地听着。"那个可亲可爱的人一定是你表兄。他是不是待你也总是那么和蔼？"

"你什么意思？"夏洛特问。

"你猜不着吗？"

---

equipment  *n.* 设备；装备                    stepson  *n.* 继子

A strange feeling came over Charlotte. "The pearls—" she started to say.

"Doesn't your cousin know either?"

Charlotte felt herself turning pink. "They're not paste?"

"Haven't you looked at them?" Mrs. Guy continued.

Charlotte felt *ashamed*. Not to have known that the pearls were real!

"Come to my room when you finish teaching," Mrs. Guy ordered, "You'll see!"

Later, in Mrs. Guy's room, Charlotte stared at the pearls around Mrs. Guy's neck. Surely they were the only *mysterious* thing her

---

夏洛特一下子产生了一种奇怪的感觉。"那些珍珠——"夏洛特开始述说起来。

"难道你表兄也不知道吗？"

夏洛特觉得自己的脸红了。"它们不是假珍珠吗？"

"你不是看了吗？"盖伊夫人接着说。

夏洛特感到很惭愧，自己居然不知道那些珍珠是真的！

"教完课到我房间里来，"盖伊夫人命令道，"你就会明白的！"

后来，在盖伊夫人的房间里，夏洛特盯着看盖伊夫人颈上戴着的珍珠。肯定，这些珍珠是她继舅妈所拥有的唯一一件神秘的东西。

---

ashamed  *adj.*  惭愧的

mysterious  *adj.*  神秘的

stepaunt had owned.

"What in the world have you done to them?"

"I only *handled* them, understood them, admired them and put them on," Mrs. Guy answered proudly. "That's what pearls need. They need to be worn—it wakes them up. They're alive, you see. How have these been treated? They must have been buried, ignored. They were half dead. Don't you know about pearls?"

"How could I have known?" said *penniless* Charlotte. "Do you?"

"I know everything about pearls. These were simply asleep. From the moment I touched them you could see they were real."

"I couldn't see," *admitted* Charlotte, "although I did wonder about

---

"你对这些珍珠究竟做了些什么？"

"我仅仅用手摸摸，把它们搞清楚，欣赏它们，然后，又戴上了。"盖伊夫人骄傲地说。"这是珍珠所需要的。它们需要有人佩戴——这样才能把它们激活。你看，它们现在都活了。你们一直是怎样对待它们的？它们一定是给埋起来了，没人理睬，已经半死了。难道你不懂得珍珠吗？"

"我怎么可能懂呢？"一贫如洗的夏洛特说。"你懂吗？"

"我对珍珠无所不知。这些珍珠仅仅是休眠。从我去摸它们的那一刻起，你都看到了，它们就活了。"

"我没看出来，"夏洛特承认说。"尽管的确有些纳闷。那么，它们

---

handle *v.* 触摸　　　　　　　　　penniless *adj.* 身无分文的
admit *v.* 承认

them. Then their value—"

"Oh, their value is *excellent*!"

Charlotte felt *dizzy*. "But my cousin didn't know. He thinks they're worthless."

"Because the rest of the jewels are false? Then your cousin is a fool. But, anyway, he gave them to you."

"But if he gave them to me because he thought they were worthless—"

"You think you must give them back? I don't agree. If he was such a fool that he didn't *recognize* their value, it's his fault."

Charlotte looked at the pearls. They were beautiful. At the moment, however, they seemed to belong more to Mrs. Guy than to

---

的价值——"

"哦，那可是太值钱了！"

夏洛特感到一阵头晕。"可我表兄并不知道。他还以为它们不值钱呢。"

"是因为其他珠宝都是假的吗？那么，你表兄就是个傻瓜。但不管怎么说，他把它们给了你。"

"可是，如果说他给我是因为他以为它们不值钱的话——"

"你觉得你必须还给他？我不赞同。如果说他都傻到这个份上，连它们的价值也看不出来的话，那就是他的错了，怪不着别人。"

夏洛特看着珍珠。它们真的很美。然而，此刻，它们看上去倒更像是盖伊夫人的，而不像是夏洛特或她表兄的。

---

excellent *adj.* 极好的        dizzy *adj.* 晕眩的
recognize *v.* 认出；承认

Charlotte or her cousin. She said finally:

"Yes, he insisted that the pearls were paste, even after I clearly said they looked different from the other things."

"Well, then, you see!" said Mrs. Guy. Her voice expressed more than *victory* over Arthur Prime—she sounded *relieved*.

But Charlotte was still not sure. "You see, he thought they couldn't be different because they shouldn't be."

"Shouldn't be? I don't understand."

"Well, how would she have got them?" Charlotte asked directly.

"Do you mean she might have stolen them?"

"No, but she had been an actress."

"Well, then!" cried Mrs. Guy. "That's exactly how she got them."

---

最后，她说："是啊，他坚持说这些珍珠是假的，甚至在我非常明确地说它们看上去与众不同的时候，他还在坚持。"

"这不就得了，你总算明白了！"盖伊夫人说。听声音，她不单是胜了亚瑟·普拉姆一筹，也是觉得放心了。

但夏洛特仍然不能肯定。"你看，他以为这些珍珠不可能有什么不同，因为它们不该有什么不同。"

"不该？我不懂。"

"我是说她到底是怎么得到的呢？"夏洛特直截了当地问。

"你的意思是说这有可能是她偷来的？"

"不。但她曾经是个演员。"

"噢，这就是了！"盖伊夫人嚷了起来。"她肯定就是这么得到的。"

---

victory *n.* 胜利

relieved *adj.* 放心的

"Yes, but she wasn't famous or rich."

"Was she ugly?" Mrs. Guy *inquired*.

"No. She must have looked rather nice when she was young."

"Well, then!" cried Mrs. Guy again, as if she had *proved* her point.

"You mean the pearls were a present? That's just the idea my cousin dislikes—that she had such a *generous* admirer."

"And that she wouldn't have taken the pearls for nothing? I should think not! Let's hope she gave him something in return. Let's hope she was kind to him."

"Well," Charlotte continued, "I suppose she must have been

---

"就算是吧，可她既不出名也不富有。"

"她长得丑吗？"盖伊夫人询问道。

"不。她年轻时一定是相当漂亮的。"

"噢，这就是了！"盖伊夫人又嚷了起来，就好像证实了自己的观点。

"你的意思是这些珍珠是一件礼物？那可正是我表兄厌恶的想法——说她有这样一个慷慨的崇拜者。"

"她不会白白接受这些珍珠吧？我认为不会！她一定是给了他什么作为回报。她一定是对他好。"

"那么，"夏洛特接着说，"我想她对他肯定是像你说的'好'。这

---

inquire *v.* 询问        prove *v.* 证明；证实

generous *adj.* 慷慨的；大方的

'kind' as you call it. That's why none of us knew she had something so valuable. That's why she had to hide them."

"You're suggesting that she was *ashamed* of them?"

"Well, she had married a minister."

"But he married her. What did he think of her past life?"

"Well, that she was not the sort of woman who *encouraged* such gifts."

"Ah!my dear! What woman is not!" said Mrs. Guy with a smile.

"And I don't want to give away her secret," continued Charlotte. "I liked her very much."

---

就是为什么我们谁都不知道她有这么宝贵的东西。这也是她不得不把它们藏起来的原因。”

"你是说她因为这些珍珠而感到羞愧？”

"呃，她嫁给了一个牧师。”

"是他把她娶回来了。他对她过去的生活是怎么看的？”

"呃，他觉得她不是那种鼓励人送这种礼物的女人。”

"哈！天哪！什么样的女人不这样啊！"盖伊夫人笑着说。

"我不想说出她的秘密，"夏洛特接着说。"我非常喜欢她。”

---

ashamed *adj.* 惭愧的 encourage *v.* 鼓励

"Then don't!" decided Mrs. Guy. "*Keep* them."

"It's so difficult!" sighed Charlotte. "I must think. I'll tell you tonight, after I decide what to do."

"But may I wear them—this evening at dinner?" Mrs. Guy's hands held the pearls lovingly.

It was probably Mrs. Guy's *possessiveness* that decided Charlotte; but for the moment she only said, "As you like," before she left the room.

It was almost eleven o'clock before Charlotte had a chance to meet with Mrs. Guy again that evening. Mrs. Guy had worn

---

"那就别说！"盖伊夫人果断地说。"把它们留下来。"

"太难了！"夏洛特叹息了一声说。"我必须好好想想。今晚等我决定了怎么办后，再告诉你。"

"那我可以戴着吗——今晚就餐的时候？"盖伊夫人的手爱惜地抚摸着那些珍珠。

也许是盖伊夫人的占有使夏洛特下了决心，但她当时只是说，"随你的便，"说完就离开了房间。

那天晚上，差不多到十一点时，夏洛特才找到机会再次见到盖伊夫人。盖伊夫人戴着珍珠吃的饭，并对夏洛特宣布说它们获得了"极大的成

---

keep *v.* 保持；保留                          possessiveness *n.* 占有

the pearls to dinner, and announced that they had been "A great success, my dear, a *sensation*!"

"They are beautiful," Charlotte agreed, "but I can't be silent."

"Then you plan to return them?"

"If I don't, I'll be a thief."

"If you do, you're a fool!" said Mrs. Guy angrily.

"Well, of the two..." Charlotte answered faintly.

Mrs. Guy *interrupted* her. "You won't tell him I told you that they're real, will you?"

"No, certainly not."

功，我亲爱的，简直是耸人听闻！"

"它们很漂亮，"夏洛特赞同地说，"但是我不能保持沉默。"

"这么说，你想还回去吗？"

"要是不还，我就是个贼。"

"要是还了，你就是个傻子！"盖伊夫人生气地说。

"嗯，在两者之间……"夏洛特含糊地说。

盖伊夫人打断了她的话。"你不会告诉他说我告诉你这些珍珠是真的吧？"

"不，当然不。"

sensation *n.* 轰动；哗然                    interrupt *v.* 打断

"Then, perhaps he won't believe you, and he will give them back to us!" And feeling much better, Mrs. Guy went to bed.

But Charlotte didn't like to return the pearls to Arthur Prime by mail, and was too busy to go to town herself. On the last day of Mrs. Guy's visit, she came to Charlotte.

"Come now, how much will you sell them for?"

"The pearls? Oh, you'll have to *bargain* with my cousin."

"Where does he live?"

Charlotte gave her the *address*.

---

"那么，他大概就不会相信你，而且还会把它们还给我们！"盖伊夫人感觉好多了，就去睡觉了。

但夏洛特不想把珍珠邮寄给亚瑟·普拉姆，而她又脱不开身进城亲自去还。那天，盖伊夫人要走了，她过来找夏洛特。

"得啦，你想卖多少钱？"

"你是说珍珠？哦，你得去跟我表兄议价。"

"他住在哪儿？"

夏洛特把地址给了她。

---

bargain  *v.*  讨价还价

address  *n.*  地址

"But how can I talk with him if you don't do anything about returning them?" Mrs. Guy *complained*.

"Oh, I will. I'm only waiting until the family goes to town. Do you want the pearls so much?"

"I'm dying for them. There's a special mystery about them. They have a white glow." Mrs. Guy *paused*. "My dear," she whispered, "they're things of love!"

"Oh, dear!" cried Charlotte.

"They're things of passion!"

"Oh, heavens!"

---

"但是，你要是按兵不动，不把珍珠还回去，我怎么跟他交涉？"盖伊夫人抱怨说。

"噢，我会还的。我只是得等这家人进城。你这么渴望这些珍珠吗？"

"渴望得要命。这些珍珠有一个特殊的秘密。它们有一种白色的光辉。"盖伊夫人停顿了一下，又小声说："亲爱的，它们是爱情的信物！"

"噢，天哪！"夏洛特喊了一声。

"它们是热恋的信物！"

"噢，天哪！"

---

complain  *v.* 抱怨

pause  *v.* 停顿

III

Mrs. Guy left, but Charlotte couldn't forget her words. She felt she had a new view of her dear, dead aunt. Had her stepaunt suffered over the pearls, hidden away with the false jewels? Charlotte began wearing the pearls *in private*; she came to feel a strange *attachment* to them. But still she was poor, and she dreamed that Arthur Prime might show an uncharacteristic generosity and say to her:

"Oh, keep the pearls! Of course, I couldn't *afford* to give them to you if I had known their value. But since you have got them, and found out the truth yourself, I really can't take them away from you."

---

III

盖伊夫人走了，但夏洛特却怎么也忘不掉她的话。她觉得她对她那亲爱的已故的舅妈有了一种新的看法。她的舅妈为了珍珠而受罪，把它们藏在假珠宝里了，会是这样吗？夏洛特开始在私下里佩戴珍珠；对它们渐渐地有了一种奇怪的依恋感。但她依然贫穷，梦想着亚瑟·普拉姆会表现出一种异常的大度，对她说：

"哦，留下那些珍珠吧！当然，如果我事先知道它们的价值的话，我肯定就不会给你了。但是，既然它们现在已经到了你手里，而且又是你自己发现了它们的价值，我实在是没法从你手里再拿回来了。"

---

in private 私下地；秘密地          attachment *n.* 依恋
afford *v.* 给予；提供

In fact, his *reaction* was quite different when she finally went to town to tell him her story.

"I don't believe in them," he said. He was angry and pale.

"That's exactly what I wanted to hear," Charlotte replied.

"It's a most unpleasant, improper suggestion," he added. "To think that she..."

"If you're afraid to believe they're real, it's not my fault."

Arthur said nothing for a while. Then he picked them up. "They're what I said *originally*. They're only paste."

"Then may I keep them?"

---

事实上，当她最终进城把事情的原委告诉表哥时，他的反应是截然不同的。

"我不相信它们是真的，"他说。气得脸色煞白。

"这正是我想听到的话，"夏洛特回答说。

"这是最令人不快的，最不合适的看法，"他又补充说。"要我认为她……"

"如果你不敢相信它们是真的，那可就怪不得我了。"

亚瑟一时间什么话也没说。然后，他把珍珠拿了起来。"还是我原先说的，不过是假的。"

"那，我还可以保留吗？"

---

reaction *n.* 反应 originally *adv.* 最初；起初

"No. I want a better *opinion*."

"Better than your opinion."

"No. Better than yours." Arthur took the pearls and locked them in a *drawer*.

"You say I'm afraid," he added. "But I won't be afraid to take them to a jeweler to ask for an opinion."

"And if he says they're real?"

"He won't say so. He couldn't," Arthur insisted.

Two weeks later Charlotte *received* a letter about the pearls from Arthur. Still later Mrs. Guy was invited to dinner by Charlotte's employer. She was wearing a beautiful string of pearls.

---

"不。我想得到更高明的见解。"

"比你的见解还要高明吗？"

"不。而是比你的见解还要高明。"亚瑟把珍珠锁进一个抽屉里。

"你说我不敢相信，"他又补充说。"但我敢把它们拿到珠宝商那去鉴定。"

"人家要说是真的呢？"

"不会这么说。不可能，"亚瑟坚持说。

两个星期后，夏洛特收到了亚瑟写来的关于珍珠的信。再后来，盖伊夫人应夏洛特雇主的邀请前来吃饭。她戴着一串漂亮的珍珠项链。

---

opinion *n.* 意见；主张

drawer *n.* 抽屉

receive *v.* 收到

"Do you see?" She came over to greet Charlotte, pointing at her necklace.

Charlotte wore a sickly smile. "They're almost as nice as Arthur's," she said.

"Almost? Where are your eyes, my dear? They are Arthur's. I tracked them to the jeweler's window where he sold them."

"Sold them?" Charlotte was *horrified*. "He wrote me that I had *insulted* his stepmother and that the jeweler had shown him that he was right—he said the pearls were only paste!"

Mrs. Guy stared at her. "Ah, I told you he wouldn't believe you."

"He wrote me," Charlotte continued, full of her private wrong,

---

她走过来跟夏洛特打招呼，用手指了指项链说："看到了吗？"

夏洛特苦笑了一下。"它们跟亚瑟的那些差不多一样美，"她说。

"差不多一样？你的眼睛呢，亲爱的？它们本来就是亚瑟的。我是在珠宝商的橱窗里看到的，他把它们卖到那里了。"

"卖了？"夏洛特非常惊骇。"他给我写信说我辱没了他的继母，说珠宝商证实他是对的——他说珍珠只不过是假货！"

盖伊夫人目不转睛地看着她。"哈，我告诉过你他不会相信你。"

"他给我写信说，"夏洛特满腹委屈地接着说，"他把它们砸碎了。"

---

horrified *adj.* 惊骇的          insult *v.* 侮辱；损害

"that he had *smashed* them."

"He is really very disturbed." Mrs. Guy's voice expressed *pity* and wonder.

But it was not quite clear whom she pitied, Arthur or Charlotte. And Charlotte felt disturbed, too, when she thought about it later. Had Mrs. Guy really tracked the pearls to a jeweler's window? Or had she dealt with Arthur directly? Charlotte remembered clearly that she had given Mrs. Guy his address.

"他的确很烦恼。"盖伊夫人的声音里有一种怜悯和惊奇。

但是,她究竟怜悯谁,是亚瑟呢,还是夏洛特,这一点并不是很清楚。夏洛特事后一想起这事也觉得很烦恼。盖伊夫人是真的寻到珠宝商那里的,还是直接跟亚瑟交易的?夏洛特清楚地记得自己曾经把他的地址给了盖伊夫人。

smash  *v.* 粉碎                                    pity  *n.* 怜悯;同情

# April Showers

Adapted from the story by Edith Wharton

Edith Newbold Jones Wharton was born in New York City in 1862. Her family was wealthy—an "old" family of New York high *society*. Edith was taught at home by *governesses*. She learned French, read widely, and traveled in Europe at an early age. In 1885 she married Teddy Wharton, a young man from an upper-class Boston family. The marriage seemed a *suitable* one, but they were not happy. Teddy did not share Edith's interests in *literature* and the arts. Three years after their marriage, Edith suffered a nervous breakdown and was unwell for about six years. Finally, in 1913, they

## 四月里的阵雨

根据伊迪丝·沃顿的同名故事改写

伊迪丝·纽博尔德·琼斯·沃顿1862年生于纽约市。她的家庭非常富有，是纽约上流社会里一户名门望族。伊迪丝的教育是跟着家庭教师完成的。她学习法语，博览群书，很小的时候就游历过欧洲。1885年，她嫁给了泰迪·沃顿，他来自上流社会的波士顿家庭。他们的婚姻看似门当户对，其实并不美满。泰迪并不像伊迪丝那样对文学和艺术感兴趣。三年后，伊迪丝患了神精失常症，一直持续了六年。1913年，

---

society *n.* 社会
suitable *adj.* 适当的；合适的

governess *n.* 女家庭教师
literature *n.* 文学

# April Showers

were divorced—an unusual, even shocking *event* at that time. By 1907 Wharton had moved to Paris and *resumed* the writing she had begun as a teenager. *The House of Mirth*(1905) was her first famous novel. Wharton died in France in 1937. She had returned to the United States just once in all those years.

But Guy's heart slept under the *violets* on Muriel's grave.

Theodora thought it was a beautiful ending. She had seen girls cry over last *chapters* that weren't half as sad as this one. She laid her pen aside and read the words again. Then, breathing deeply, she wrote across the bottom of the page the name she would use in literature—Gladys Glyn.

---

他们的婚姻宣告结束，成为当时轰动一时的非常事件。到了1907年，沃顿移居巴黎，并恢复了早在少年时代就开始的写作生涯。长篇小说《欢乐之家》（1905）是她的成名作。沃顿1937年逝世于法国。远在异国他乡的那些年里，她仅回美国一次。

但年轻人的心在穆里尔坟墓上盛开的紫罗兰下睡着了。

西奥多拉认为这是一个美丽的结局。她在前几章里就见过女孩子们哭泣，但那种哭泣的悲伤程度与这种哀痛相比真的是连一半也不及。她把笔放到一边又重新读起那些话来。接着，她深吸了一口气，在书页的底部写上了她的笔名：格拉迪丝·格林。

---

event *n.* 事件；大事　　　　　　　　resume *v.* 重新开始
violet *n.* 紫罗兰　　　　　　　　　　chapter *n.* 章节

Downstairs the clock struck two. Two o'clock in the morning! And Theodora had *promised* her mother to be up early to sew buttons on Johnny's jacket, and to make sure that Kate and Bertha took their cod-liver oil before school!

Slowly, tenderly, she gathered up the pages of her *manuscript*. There were five hundred of them. She tied them together with a blue satin *ribbon*. Her Aunt Julia had given the ribbon to her. She had wanted to wear it with her new white dress on Sunday. But this was a much nobler use for it. She tied the ends of the ribbon in a pretty bow. Theodora was clever at making bows. She could have *been good at* decorating things, but she gave all her spare time to

---

楼下的时钟正敲两点。凌晨两点！西奥多拉答应过母亲要早起为约翰尼的夹克衫缝纽扣，还要保证凯特和贝莎在上学前把鱼肝油吞下肚去！

她缓缓地、轻柔地把手稿收集起来。那是整整五百页的手稿。她用一条蓝色的缎带把这些稿页捆扎好，那条缎带是她姨妈朱丽娅送的，她一直想在礼拜日穿那条新的白裙子时再佩戴，现在把它用到这上可就显得高贵多了。她把缎带的两端打成一个蝴蝶结。她很会打蝴蝶结，本来很擅长搞装饰，但把所有的闲暇时间都用到文学上了。这时，她又最后看了一眼前

---

promise *v.* 允诺；许诺
ribbon *n.* 带；缎带

manuscript *n.* 手稿
be good at 擅长做……

literature. Then, with a last look at the precious pages, she closed and addressed the package. She would send it off next morning to *Home Circle*. She knew it would be hard to get *published* in this magazine, with all its popular *authors*. But she had been encouraged to try by her Uncle James.

Uncle James had been visiting from Boston, to tell them about his new house. "And who do you think is our new neighbor?" He smiled at Theodora. "Probably you know all about her. Ever hear of Kathleen Kyd?"

Kathleen Kyd!She thought with *admiration*. The famous *novelist*, author of more popular romances than all the other authors put together! The author of *Fashion and Passion*, *An American Duchess*, and *Rhona's Revolt*! Was there an intelligent girl from Maine to California whose heart would not beat faster at the sound of that

---

面的几页，然后才合拢起来，开始写邮件地址。她得赶在明天上午把邮件寄给《家庭》杂志。她知道在这家杂志发表作品绝非易事，因为这家杂志所刊登的都是名人的作品。但她的叔叔詹姆斯促使她碰碰运气。

那次詹姆斯叔叔从波士顿来访是想告诉他们他新近搬家的事。"你知道是谁跟我们做邻居了吗？"他微笑着问西奥多拉。"你大概非常熟悉她。听说过凯瑟琳·基德吗？"

凯瑟琳·基德！她满怀敬仰地想着。那不是著名的小说家吗？那个以写浪漫作品著称的作家，她比所有的作家加在一起还要浪漫！她写过《时尚与激情》、《一位美国公爵夫人》和《罗娜的反叛》！从东部的缅因州到西部的加州，有哪个有才智的女孩一听到这个名字会不为之心驰神往？

---

publish *v.* 出版；发行
admiration *n.* 钦佩；美慕

author *n.* 作者
novelist *n.* 小说家

name?

"Why, yes," Uncle James was saying. "Kathleen Kyd lives next door. Frances G. Wallop is her real name, and her husband's a *dentist*. She's a very pleasant kind of woman—you'd never know she was a writer. Ever hear how she began to write? She told me the whole story. It seems she was a *saleswoman* in a store, earning practically nothing. She had to support her mother and her sister, who's *helplessly* handicapped. Well, she wrote a story one day, just for fun, and sent it to *Home Circle*. They'd never heard of her, of course, and she never expected to hear from them. She did, though. They took her story and asked for more. She became a regular *contributor*. Now she tells me her books bring her in about ten thousand dollars a year." He smiled ironically at Theodora's father. "That's rather more than you or I make, eh, John? I certainly hope

---

　　"哎呀，是啊，"詹姆斯叔叔还在说着。"凯瑟琳·基德就住在隔壁。她的真名叫弗朗西斯·沃洛普。她丈夫是个牙医。她是那种非常令人愉快的女人。你根本看不出她竟是一位作家。知道她是怎样开始写作的吗？她把什么都告诉我了。她从前好像是商店里的售货员，其实挣不到什么钱，但得养活母亲和有残疾的妹妹。有一天，她写了一篇故事，不过是写着玩，就寄到《家庭》去了。当然，人家从来没听说过她，而她也根本没指望会得到答复。但结果却是真的给她答复了。他们把这故事发表出来，还要求她再写一些。这样，她就成了固定撰稿人。她告诉我说书可以给她带来一万美元的年收入。"他笑了笑，不无嘲讽地看着西奥多拉的父亲，说："这可比你我都挣得多啊，约翰。我当然希望咱们这个家门不要

---

dentist *n.* 牙科医生　　　　　　　　saleswoman *n.* 女售货员
helplessly *adv.* 无助地；无能为力地　　contributor *n.* 投稿人

this household doesn't contribute to her support." He looked sharply at Theodora. "I don't believe in feeding young people on *sentimental* romances!"

Theodora listened *breathlessly*. Kathleen Kyd's first story had been accepted by *Home Circle* and they had asked for more. Why should Gladys Glyn be less fortunate? Theodora had done a lot of romance reading—far more than her parents were aware of. She felt she could *judge* the quality of her own work. She was almost sure that her novel, *April Showers*, was a fine book. Perhaps it lacked Kathleen Kyd's tender humor. But it had an *emotional* depth that Kyd never reached. Theodora did not care to amuse her readers—she would leave that to less serious authors. Her aim was to stir the

出现给她捧场的人。"说着，他还用严厉的目光扫了一眼西奥多拉。"我就是不主张给年轻人灌输那些多愁善感的浪漫玩意儿！"

西奥多拉平心静气地听着。凯瑟琳·基德的第一个故事已经被《家庭》接受了，而且还跟她约更多的稿件。为什么格拉迪丝·格林就没那么幸运呢？西奥多拉读过那么多浪漫故事——远远超过她父母所意识到的。她觉得自己有能力评判自己作品的质量。她几乎可以肯定她的长篇小说《四月里的阵雨》是一部佳作，里面也许缺少凯瑟琳·基德那亲切的幽默，但却有一种基德永远也达不到的感情深度。西奥多拉并不想取悦读者，她认为取悦读者的事是那些不甚严肃的作家的事。她的创作意图就是

sentimental *adj.* 感伤的
judge *v.* 判断；断定

breathlessly *adv.* 屏息地；气喘地
emotional *adj.* 感情（上）的

depths of human emotion, and she felt she had succeeded. It was a great thing for a girl to feel that about her first novel. Theodora was only seventeen—she remembered with a touch of pity that the great author George Eliot had not become famous until she was nearly forty.

No, there was no doubt that *April Showers* was a fine novel. But would a less fine book have a better chance to be published? Would it be wiser to write the book down to the *average* reader's level, and save for a future novel the great emotion that she had written into this book? No! Never would she change her words to suit *ignorant* taste!The great authors never sank to such tricks—nor would she. The manuscript should be sent as it was.

---

激发人类心灵深处的情感。现在，她感觉自己已经成功了。一个女孩子对自己的第一部作品能有如此感觉，实在是一件很了不起的事情。西奥多拉才十七岁——她略感遗憾地记得伟大作家乔治·艾略特将近四十岁时才成名成家。

《四月里的阵雨》，毫无疑问，是一本好书。就算不那么好，那么，就不该有机会出版吗？如果先写一部低于一般读者水平的书，而把已经写进这部作品中的伟大情感留起来以备将来再写一部是不是更明智一些呢？不！她绝不改变自己的话语以迎合愚昧无知的欣赏口味！伟大的作家从不降低到玩弄这种伎俩的地步，她也绝对不会。手稿一定要按原定计划寄出去。

---

average *adj.* 平均的；普通的        ignorant *adj.* 无知的；愚昧的

Theodora woke up suddenly, worried. What was it? *Home Circle* had refused *April Showers*? No, that couldn't be it. There lay the precious manuscript, waiting to be mailed. Ah, it was the clock downstairs, striking nine o'clock. It was Johnny's buttons, and the girls to get ready!

Theodora jumped out of bed feeling *guilty*. She didn't want to disappoint her mother about the buttons. Her mother was handicapped by *rheumatism*, and had to give much of the care of the household to her oldest daughter. Theodora honestly meant to see that Johnny had all his buttons sewed back on, and that Kate and Bertha went to school tidy. Unfortunately, the writing of a great novel leaves little time or *memory* for the small *responsibilities*. Theodora

---

　西奥多拉突然醒来，感到有些担忧。怎么回事？《家庭》杂志拒绝了《四月里的阵雨》？不，这不可能。那宝贵的手稿还在那里，静静地等着寄出。哦，是楼下的钟声正敲九点。该给约翰尼缝纽扣了，还有，得让妹妹们准备上学了！

　西奥多拉从床上一跃而起，心里感觉很愧疚。她不想因纽扣的事让母亲失望。母亲患有风湿病，不得不把大部分家务活交给她这个大女儿来做。西奥多拉真心地想看到约翰尼的纽扣都已缝好，凯特和贝莎也都穿戴整齐地上学了。然而，遗憾的是，要想写一部大书就没有时间顾及或干脆忘记履行一些小小的责任。西奥多拉发现自己的好意通常来不及付诸实

---

guilty *adj.* 内疚的；有罪的　　　　rheumatism *n.* 风湿病
memory *n.* 记忆　　　　　　　　responsibility *n.* 责任；职责

usually found that her good intentions came too late for practical results.

Her guilt was softened by the thought that literary success would make up for all her little failings. She intended to spend all her money on her family. Already she could see the *wheel chair* she would buy for her mother, and the fresh *wallpaper* for her father's office. She would buy *bicycles* for the girls, and send Johnny to a boarding school where someone else would sew on his buttons. If her parents could have guessed her intentions, they would not *blame* her for her failings. And her father, on this particular morning, would not have looked up to say, in his weary, ironic way.

"I suppose you didn't get home from the dance till morning?"

---

施，所以也就见不到什么实效。

想到文学创作的成功会弥补她的小小失误，负疚感也就减轻了。她打算把自己的钱全部拿出来贴补家用。她在脑海里已经能够看见那辆要买给母亲的轮椅了，还看到了为父亲办公室购置的新墙纸。她要给两个妹妹各买一辆自行车，还要送约翰尼去一所能有人为他缝纽扣的寄宿学校。假如她的父母能猜出她的打算来，他们就不会因为她的失职而责怪她了。她的父亲，在这个非同寻常的早晨，也就不会抬起头来，以他那种厌倦的、讽刺的方式说：

"你该不是出去跳舞到早晨才回来吧？"

---

wheel chair 轮椅
bicycle *n.* 自行车

wallpaper *n.* 壁纸；墙纸
blame *v.* 责备

Theodora's sense of good intentions helped her take her father's *criticism* calmly.

"I'm sorry to be late, father," she said. Her *tenderness* would have quieted a parent in fiction, but Dr. Dace never behaved like a father in a book.

"Your *apology* shows your good manners," he said *impatiently*, "but manners won't keep your mother's breakfast warm."

"Hasn't mother's tray gone up yet?"

"Who was to take it, I'd like to know? The girls came down so late that I had to hurry them off before they'd finished breakfast. And Johnny's hands were so dirty that I sent him back to his room to clean up. It's a fine thing when the doctor's children are the dirtiest children in town!"

---

西奥多拉心中所怀的好意帮助她平静地接受了父亲的批评。

"很抱歉，父亲，我起来晚了，"她说。她的温柔可以平息小说里一位父亲的恼火，但戴斯医生绝对不会像书中描写的那种父亲。

"你的道歉说明你还挺有礼貌，"他不耐烦地说，"但礼貌并不能让你母亲的早餐保温。"

"母亲的餐盘还没端上楼吗？"

"谁给端呢？我倒很想知道。那两个女孩下来得那么晚，她们还没吃完早饭就被我给匆匆打发走了。约翰尼的手那么脏，我让他回自己房间里去洗洗。医生的孩子成了全城最脏的孩子，这倒不错啊！"

---

criticism *n.* 批评　　　　　　　　tenderness *n.* 亲切；柔软
apology *n.* 道歉　　　　　　　　impatiently *adv.* 无耐性地

Theodora quickly *prepared* her mother's tray, leaving her own breakfast untouched. As she entered the room upstairs her mother smiled tenderly at her. But Mrs. Dace's *patience* was harder to bear than Dr. Dace's criticism.

"Mother, I'm so sorry—"

"No matter, dear. I suppose Johnny's buttons kept you. I can't think what that boy does to his clothes!"

"Theodora set the tray down without answering. She couldn't talk about her *forgetfulness* without giving away the cause of it. For a few weeks longer she would have to be misunderstood. Then—ah, then, if her novel was accepted, how gladly she would forget and forgive misunderstanding! But what if it were refused? She turned away from her mother to hide her worry. Well, if it was *refused*, she

---

西奥多拉迅速地准备好母亲的餐盘，而她自己的早餐却连一口也没动。当她上楼来到母亲的房间时，母亲对她温柔地笑了。然而，戴斯夫人的忍耐比戴斯先生的批评更让人难以忍受。

"母亲，真是太抱歉了——"

"没关系，亲爱的。我猜想是约翰尼的纽扣耽误了你，真想不出这孩子怎么会把衣服穿成这样！"

西奥多拉默默地放下餐盘。她觉得只要一说起自己的疏忽大意，就得讲出个缘由来。她遭受误解也就是几个星期的事了。然后，哈，然后，假如她的小说被接受了的话，那么，她就会多么乐意忘却并宽恕这种误解啊！但如果这书被拒绝了该怎么办？她转过身去不想让母亲看到自己的担忧。那么，假如书稿被拒绝了，她就会请求父母原谅她。她就会心安理得

---

prepare *v.* 准备
forgetfulness *n.* 健忘

patience *n.* 耐心；忍耐
refuse *v.* 拒绝

would ask her parents to *forgive* her. She would settle down without complaining to a wasted life of sewing and cod-liver oil.

Theodora had said to herself that after the manuscript had been sent off, she would have time to look after the children. But she hadn't thought about the *mailman*. He came three times a day. For an hour before each visit, she was too excited to work, wondering if he would bring an answer this time. And for an hour after he left she moved about in a heavy cloud of disappointment. Meanwhile, the children had never been so difficult. They seemed always to be coming to pieces like cheap *furniture*. Mrs. Dace worried herself ill over Johnny's clothes, Bertha's bad marks at school, and Kate's *refusal* to take her cod-liver oil. And Dr. Dace came home late

---

地、毫无怨言地在那种给弟妹缝纽扣和吃鱼肝油的琐事中打发时光。

手稿寄走后，西奥多拉曾经自言自语地说她就会有时间照看弟妹了。但她并没有想到那个邮差，他可是一天来三次的啊。每次邮差来的前一个小时，她都激动得无法干活，心里琢磨着他这次会不会给他带来答复。邮差走后，又得有一个小时的时间，她的心头笼罩着极度失望的阴云，她走来走去，坐立不安。与此同时，孩子们也变得从未有过的难以对付，总是像破家具一样散了架。戴斯夫人为约翰尼的衣服担心得要命；贝莎在学校的成绩太糟；凯特拒不服用鱼肝油；戴斯医生巡诊晚归后发现壁炉冰凉，

---

forgive *v.* 原谅
furniture *n.* 家具

mailman *n.* 邮差
refusal *n.* 拒绝

from visiting his patients to find a cold *fireplace* and nothing to eat. He called angrily for Theodora to come downstairs and take the embroidered words, "East, West, Home is Best" down off the wall.

The week was a long *nightmare*. Theodora could neither eat nor sleep. She was up early enough. But instead of taking care of the children and making breakfast, she wandered down the street to meet the mailman. Then she would come back empty-handed, forgetting her morning responsibilities. She had no idea how long she would be *forced* to wait, but she didn't see how authors could live if they were kept waiting more than a week.

Then, suddenly, one evening—she never knew how or when it happened—she found herself with a *Home Circle envelope* in her

---

食物皆无。他生气地把西奥多拉喊下楼来，让她把那条刺绣的条幅"走南闯北，家里最美"从墙上摘下来。

整整一个星期就是一个长长的噩梦。西奥多拉吃不下，睡不着。每天早晨，她都早早起床，但不是照料弟弟妹妹，也不是准备早餐，而是到街上徘徊，想要遇见邮差。走够了，就两手空空地回来，完全忘记了早晨那些应该做的事情。她根本不知道还得等待多久，不明白如果让那些作家的等待超过一个星期的话，他们还怎么能够活得下去。

突然，有一天晚上——她根本就闹不清是怎么回事儿，事情就发生了——她发现自己手里正握着一个装有《家庭》杂志的信封。她的目光急

---

fireplace *n.* 壁炉
force *v.* 强迫

nightmare *n.* 噩梦
envelope *n.* 信封

hand. Her eyes flashed over the letter—a wild dance of words that wouldn't settle down and make sense.

"Dear Madam:" (They called her Madam!) And then, yes, the words were beginning to fall into line now. "Your novel, *April Showers*, has been received, and we are glad to *accept* it on the usual terms. Chapters of a novel we were planning to start publishing were delayed due to the author's illness. The first chapter of *April Showers* will therefore appear in our *midsummer* edition. Thanking you for sending this contribution, *Sincerely* yours..." and so forth.

Theodora ran outside into the spring evening. Spring!Everything was crowding toward the light, and in her own heart, hundreds

---

速地扫视着信件的内容——可是，那些字好像在疯狂地跳跃，怎么也不能安分下来，实在令人难以辨认。

"亲爱的夫人："（他们称她为夫人！）接着，好些了，那些字现在开始排行列队了。"您的小说《四月里的阵雨》可以出版。我们很高兴按惯例接受它。我们有一部马上就要出版的小说因作者生病，不得不拖延一些章节。这样，《四月里的阵雨》第一章将刊登在仲夏版上。谢谢您的投稿。您真诚的……"，等等。

西奥多拉一下子跑到外面，融入了春光明媚的暮色之中。啊，春天！万物齐聚，涌向光明。在她自己的心中，无数的希望在发芽长叫。透过树

---

accept *v.* 接受；承认　　　　　　midsummer *n.* 仲夏；盛夏
sincerely *adv.* 真诚地

of hopes burst into leaf. She looked up through the trees at the tender moon. She felt surrounded by an *atmosphere* of loving understanding. The brown earth was full of joy. The *treetops* moved with joy. A joyous star burst through the branches, as if to say, "I know!"

Theodora, on the whole, behaved very well. Her mother cried, her father whistled, and said (but less ironically than usual) that he supposed he'd never get a hot meal again. And the children added noisily to this *unfamiliar*, *joyous* scene.

Within a week, everybody in town knew that Theodora had written a novel, and that it was coming out in *Home Circle*. Other girls copied her way of dressing and speaking. The local newspaper

---

枝仰望天空温柔的月亮，她感到自己被融融的爱意和理解包围着，棕色的大地充满了喜悦。树冠因为喜悦而摇曳婆娑，一颗欢欣雀跃的星星透过树枝朝下窥望，好像在说："我知道了！"

西奥多拉从总体上说表现得还算优雅得体。而她的母亲却哭了，父亲吹起了口哨，说（但已经不像以往那样尖刻了）感觉自己好像再也没有吃过一顿热乎饭菜。孩子们也闹哄哄地融入这种以前很少见过的喜庆场面中来。

在一星期之内，全城的人都知道西奥多拉写了一部小说，而且是刊登在《家庭》杂志上。别的女孩开始效仿她的衣着和言行；当地的报纸约她

---

atmosphere *n.* 气氛　　　　　　　　　　　　　treetop *n.* 树梢
unfamiliar *adj.* 不熟悉的；不常见的　　　　　joyous *adj.* 充满欢乐的

asked her for a *poem*. Her old school teachers stopped to shake her hand, and shyly *congratulated* her. Uncle James even came down from Boston to talk about her success. From what Kathleen Kyd told him, he thought Theodora would probably get a thousand dollars for her story. He suggested that she should give him the money to buy shares in a company he *was interested in*, and suggested a plot for her next romance.

Theodora waited impatiently for the midsummer *Home Circle*— and at last the great day came. Before the book store opened, Theodora was waiting on the sidewalk to buy the midsummer *Home Circle*. She ran home without opening the precious magazine. Her *excitement* was almost more than she could bear. Not hearing her

---

写诗；她从前学校里的老师在路上停下脚步同她握手，还羞涩地向她表示祝贺。詹姆斯叔叔甚至专程从波士顿赶来谈论她的成功。他从凯瑟琳·基德从前对他说过的话里判断，认为写这部小说大概会赚一千美元。他建议她把钱交给他来购买他感兴趣的一家公司的股份，还给她提供了一个创作下一部浪漫小说的情节。

　　西奥多拉焦心地等待着仲夏版的《家庭》杂志。终于，那个伟大的时刻来到了。还没等书店开门营业，西奥多拉就在人行道上等候购买仲夏版的《家庭》了。她捧着没有启封的珍贵杂志跑回家里，激动之情简直无法承受。她没听见父亲喊她吃早饭，径直跑到楼上，把自己锁进房间里。她

---

poem n. 诗
be interested in 对……感兴趣

congratulate v. 祝贺；恭喜
excitement n. 兴奋；刺激

father call her to breakfast, she ran upstairs and locked herself in her room. Her hands shook so that she could hardly turn the pages. At last—yes, there it was: *April Showers.*

The magazine dropped from her hands. What name had she read beneath the title? Had her emotion blinded her?

"*April Showers*, by Kathleen Kyd"

Kathleen Kyd! Oh, cruel *misprint*! Oh, careless editor! Through tears of furious disappointment, Theodora looked again. Yes, she had made no mistake—it was that *hateful* name. She found herself reading a *paragraph* that she had never seen before. She read farther. It was all strange. The truth burst upon her: it was not her story!

---

双手颤抖着，几乎无法翻页。总算翻开了——哦，就是这里，明明白白地写着：《四月里的阵雨》。

　　杂志从她的手中滑落到地上。标题下面的署名是什么？是激动的情绪蒙蔽了她的双眼吗？

　　"《四月里的阵雨》，作者凯瑟琳·基德"

　　凯瑟琳·基德！天哪，多么残酷的印刷错误！噢，粗心大意的编辑呀！透过极度失望的泪眼，重新审视一遍，没错——正是那个可恶的名字。她不知不觉地读了一段，那是她以前从未读过的一段话。她又接着往下读。那些话完全是陌生的。她一下子明白了真相：那不是她写的故事！

---

misprint *n.* 印刷错误
paragraph *n.* 段落

hateful *adj.* 可恶的；可憎的

It was hours later. Theodora never knew how she had got back to the Boston train *station*. She had *struggled* through the crowd, and was pushed into the train. It would be dark when she got home, but that didn't matter. Nothing mattered now. She sank into her *seat*, and closed her eyes. She tried to shut out what had happened in the last few hours, but minute by minute her memory forced her to *relive* the experience.

Although she didn't know Boston well, she had made her way easily enough to the *Home Circle* building. At least, she supposed she had. She remembered nothing until she found herself going up the stairs as easily as one does unbelievable things in dreams. She must have been walking fast, for her heart was beating furiously. She barely had breath to whisper the editor's name to the young man

---

　　几个小时过去了。西奥多拉根本不知道她是怎么回到波士顿火车站的。她曾经奋力穿过拥挤的人群，又被拥入火车车厢。她知道待她回来时天肯定黑了，但她并不介意。她已经对什么事都不介意了。她一下子跌进座位里，闭上了双眼。试图排遣几个小时以来所发生的一切，但她的记忆却一步步逼着她重温这段不幸的经历。

　　她虽然不很熟悉波士顿，但她还是比较容易地找到了《家庭》杂志社所在的楼房。至少，她觉得不难。她在上楼，上楼之前的事她全都不记得了。她发觉自己上楼就像在睡梦中做那些令人难以置信的事情一样轻而易举。她肯定是走得很快，因为她的心在狂跳不已。她对那位接待她的年轻

---

station *n.* 站；车站
seat *n.* 座位

struggle *v.* 艰难地进行
relive *v.* 重温；回味

who met her. He led her to an inner office which seemed filled by a huge force. Theodora felt herself overpowered, *conquered* by this force—she could hardly speak or hear.

Gradually, words floated up around her. "*April Showers*, Mrs. Kyd's new novel? Your manuscript, you say? You have a letter from me? The name, please? It must be some unfortunate misunderstanding. One moment." And then a bell was ringing, the young man was unlocking a *cupboard*, and the manuscript, her own precious manuscript, tied with Aunt Julia's ribbon, was laid on the table before her. Her stream of angry questions was drowned in a flood of pleasant apology: "An unfortunate accident—Mrs. Kyd's manuscript received the same day—how strange you chose the same title—two *acceptance* letters sent by *mistake*—Miss Dace's novel

---

人轻声说出编辑的名字时简直喘不过气来了。他把她带进里间的办公室，那里似乎充满了一种巨大的压力。西奥多拉觉得自己被这种压力压倒了，征服了——简直说不出一句话，也听不见一个字。

最后总算有一些字眼从她周身冒了出来：“《四月里的阵雨》，基德夫人的新作？你们说是你们的手稿？你们收到我的信了吗？请问是什么名字？这里一定有什么令人遗憾的误会。等一下。”这时，听到一声铃响，是那年轻人在开橱柜的锁。接着，手稿，那属于她自己的珍贵的手稿，那用朱丽娅姨妈的缎带系着的手稿，摆到了她面前的桌子上。她那一连串生气的问题完全被一大堆轻松的道歉给淹没了：“一个令人遗憾的事故——基德夫人的稿件是在同一天收到的——你们居然选用了同一个书名，真是太奇怪了——两封回信阴差阳错——戴斯小姐的小说不合要求——当然就

---

conquer *v.* 战胜；克服　　　　　cupboard *n.* 橱柜
acceptance *n.* 接受；接纳　　　　mistake *n.* 错误

didn't suit their needs—should, of course, have been returned —so sorry—accidents would happen—sure she understood—."

The voice *went on*. When it stopped, Theodora found herself in the street. A taxi nearly ran her over. A car honked in her ears. She held her manuscript tenderly in the crowd, like a live thing that had been hurt. She could not bear to look at its soiled *edges*, and the *ink* spot on Aunt Julia's ribbon.

The train stopped suddenly. It was her stop. She saw other passengers getting off and she followed them into the *darkness*. A warm wind blew into her face the smell of summer woods. She thought back to the spring when she had been so full of joy. Then

---

得退稿——很抱歉——出了这种事故——相信你能理解——。"

　　道歉的声音还在继续。当这声音再也听不见的时候，西奥多拉发觉自己已经走在大街上了。一辆出租车差点撞着她。还有一辆轿车与她擦身而过。她走在人群中，温柔地抱着自己的手稿，就好像那是一只受伤的生灵。她不忍看着它那被弄脏的页边，还有朱丽娅姨妈缎带上那滴红色的墨水印记。

　　火车突然停下，到站了，她该下车了。她看到其他乘客鱼贯而下，她也随着人群走入了茫茫的夜色中。暖风迎面扑来，带过一股夏天树林的味道。她想起了那个让她满怀喜悦的春日。接着，她才想起了家。她一清早

---

go on 继续
ink *n.* 墨水

edge *n.* 边缘；边界
darkness *n.* 黑暗

she thought of home. She had run out in the morning without a word. Her heart sank at the thought of her mother's fears. And her father—how angry he would be! She *bent* her head under the coming storm of his criticism.

The night was cloudy, and as she stepped into the darkness a hand was slipped into hers. She stood still, too *weary* to feel frightened. A voice said, quietly:

"Don't walk so fast, child. You look tired."

"Father!You were at the station?" she whispered.

"It's such a good night, I thought I'd *wander* down and meet you."

---

就一言不发地离开了家。想到母亲的担忧，心不禁为之一沉。还有她的父亲——他该有多么生气！她在即将到来的劈头盖脸的呵斥面前低下了头。

夜晚的天空布满了阴云，她正要举步迈进那茫茫的漆黑之中，一只手伸过来抓住了她的手。她一下子站住了，但她疲惫不堪，已经感觉不到惊恐了。这时，一个声音说话了，语调很平静。

"孩子，不要走得太快，你看上去太累了。"

"父亲！你在车站？"她小声说。

"今晚天气好，我就想随便走走，也好接接你。"

---

bend *v.* 弯曲

wander *v.* 漫步

weary *adj.* 疲倦的

She could not see his face in the darkness, but the light of his *cigar* looked down on her like a friendly eye. She took *courage* to say, "Then you knew—"

"That you'd gone to Boston? Well, I thought you probably had."

They walked on slowly, and then he added, "You see, you left the *Home Circle* lying in your room."

How she blessed the dark sky! She couldn't have borne even the tiniest star to look at her. "Then Mother wasn't much frightened?"

"Why, no, she didn't seem to be. She's been busy all day over some sewing for Bertha."

Theodora's voice was *choked* with tears. "Father, I'll—" She

---

她在黑暗中看不见他的面孔，但他嘴里的雪茄却像一只友善的眼睛在俯视着她。她鼓起勇气说："这么说，你知道——"

"知道你去了波士顿？嗯，我猜你大概是去了。"

他们慢慢地走着。他又补充说："你知道吗，你把《家庭》落在房间里了。"

多亏这漆黑的夜空啊！此时此刻，哪怕有最微小的星星躲在远方的天际看着她，她也将无法忍受。"那么，母亲没有太吓着吧？"

"怎么会呢？没有，她好像并没有感到害怕。一整天都在忙着给贝莎缝衣服。"

西奥多拉的声音有些哽咽。"父亲，我——"她在极力搜索恰当的

---

cigar *n.* 雪茄　　　　　　　　　　　courage *n.* 勇气；胆量
choke *v.* 哽噎；窒息

reached for words, but they escaped her. "I'll do things—differently; I haven't meant—" Suddenly she heard herself bursting out: "It was all a mistake, you know—about my story. They didn't want it; they won't have it!" She couldn't bear his *amusement*.

She felt his *arm* around her, and was sure he was laughing. But they moved on in silence. Then he said:

"It hurts a bit just at first, doesn't it?"

"Oh, Father!"

He stood still a *moment*, and the light of his cigar shone on his face. "You see, I've been through it myself."

"You, Father? You?"

---

词汇，但此时却连一个也找不到。"我要做事——做别的事情；我并不是想——"突然，她听到自己一下子哭出声来："事情全错了，你知道——就是我的小说。他们没要，而且将来也不想要！"她无法忍受他的发笑。

她感到他用胳膊搂着她，所以，可以肯定，他是在笑。但他们还是默默地往前走。这时，他说：

"开始的时候有点难受，是吧？"

"哦，父亲！"

他一下站住了，嘴里的雪茄照亮了他的脸。"你瞧，我本人也经历过这种事。"

"你，父亲？你？"

---

amusement  *n.*  可笑；娱乐          arm  *n.*  手臂

moment  *n.*  瞬间

"Why, yes. Didn't I ever tell you? I wrote a novel once. I was just out of *college*, and didn't want to be a doctor. No; I wanted to be a *brilliant* writer. So I wrote a novel."

The doctor paused, and Theodora held fast to his arm in silent *sympathy*. It was as if a drowning creature caught a live hand in the murderous fury of the waves.

"It took me a year—a whole year's hard work. When I'd finished, no publisher would have it, not at any price. That's why I came to meet you, because I remembered my walk home."

---

"怎么？当然。难道我没告诉过你吗？我曾经写过一部小说。那时，我刚从大学毕业，不想当医生。一点都不想。我就想当个有才华的作家。所以，就写了一部小说。"

医生顿住了。西奥多拉在默默无语的同情中紧紧地握住了他的胳膊，就好像一个即将溺死的生灵在凶险的波涛中抓住了一只救生的手。

"我用了一年的时间——整整一年的时间写这本书。写完之后，没有一个出版商想要出版它，不管付出什么价码。我今晚之所以来接你，就是因为我还记得那天晚上走回家的情景。"

---

college *n.* 大学；学院
sympathy *n.* 同情

brilliant *adj.* 杰出的；有才华的

# Rip Van Winkle

Adapted from the story by Washington Irving

Washington Irving was the first person born in America to succeed as a *professional* writer. He was the first widely read American writer of short stories and became the first American to win *recognition* in Europe for his *literary* work. Irving was born in 1783 in New York City, the youngest of eleven children. His wealthy parents named him for General George Washington, who led the American army during the Revolutionary War (1775—1781) and later became the first *president* of the United States. In 1819, while he

---

# 李普·范·温克尔

根据华盛顿·欧文的同名故事改写

华盛顿·欧文是第一位在美国本土上出生的职业作家。他是第一位以短篇小说见长从而拥有广泛读者的美国作家，也是第一位以文学作品赢得欧洲承认的美国人。欧文1783年生于纽约市，是家里十一个孩子中最小的。他的父母十分富有，以华盛顿将军的名字为他命名。华盛顿将军在美国革命战争（1775—1781）时期统领美国军队，后来又成为美国第一任总统。1819年，他在旅英期间发表了《见闻杂

---

professional *adj.* 职业的；专业的
literary *adj.* 文学的

recognition *n.* 承认；认可
president *n.* 总统

was living in England, he published *A Sketch Book*, which *includes* two famous stories, *The Legend of Sleepy Hollow* and *Rip Van Winkle*. He returned to Europe *frequently* during his long life, and for three years he was the American *ambassador* to Spain. One of Irving's last works was *The Life of Washington*, which he *considered* his finest book. Soon after completing it, he died at Sunnyside—his home on the Hudson River in New York State—in 1859.

Whoever has made a voyage up the Hudson River must remember the Catskill mountains. They are seen away to the west of the river, rising up to a noble height. Every change of season, every change of weather, indeed every hour of the day, produces some change in their magical colors and shapes.

At the foot of these mountains the voyager may have noticed the

记》，其中收录了两个著名的故事：《睡谷的传说》及《李普·范·温克尔》。在漫长的一生中，他经常重返欧洲，其中有三年时间，还出任美国驻西班牙大使。在欧文的晚年作品中，有一部《华盛顿略传》，他自认为是其最佳作品。这部作品完成后不久，就在家乡——纽约州哈德孙河上的向阳坡与世长辞了，时值1859年。

凡是沿哈德孙河做上游航行的人都一定会记得凯兹盖尔山脉。它们高耸于该河西岸。随着季节的更迭、天气的变化，甚至在一天里的不同时刻，它们神奇的色彩和形状都会发生某种变化。

在山脚下，航行者也许会注意到那袅袅的轻烟从树林中的村庄蜿蜒飘

include *v.* 包含；包括        frequently *adv.* 频繁地；经常地
ambassador *n.* 大使；代表       consider *v.* 认为；考虑

light smoke curving upwards from a village set among the trees. It is a little village of great age. It was built by Dutch *colonists* in early times. The houses were made of small yellow bricks brought from *Holland*, and they were built in the old style of Dutch country houses.

In that same village, and in one of those very houses (which to tell the exact truth was sadly time-worn and weather-beaten), there lived a simple *good-natured* fellow named Rip Van Winkle. This was many years ago, when the country was still a colony of Great Britain. Even before that, the Van Winkle family had served *bravely* in the army of the Dutch Governor, Peter Stuyvesant. Rip, however, was not blessed with his family's war-like character. I have said that he was a simple good-natured fellow; he was moreover a kind neighbor and an obedient, henpecked husband. Indeed, the mildness of spirit

---

出。那是一座古老的小村庄，还是荷兰殖民者在早期建立起来的。房屋是用从荷兰带来的小块黄砖搭建的，样式古朴，具有古老的荷兰乡村房屋风格。

在这座小村庄里的这类房屋中有那么一座（实话实说，已经饱经岁月沧桑，历尽风雨侵蚀，变得陈旧不堪），里面住着一个头脑简单的好脾气的人，他的名字叫李普·范·温克尔。这是许多年前的事了。那时，这个国家还是大英帝国的殖民地。在此之前，范·温克尔家族曾有人在荷兰统治者彼得·斯特伊弗桑特的军队中英勇作战。然而，李普却不具备其家族的尚武性格。我已经说过，他是一个头脑简单的好脾气的人，更是一个好邻居和一个听话的、怕老婆的丈夫。的确，他温文尔雅的气质使他

---

colonist *n.* 殖民者
good-natured *adj.* 好脾气的

Holland *n.* 荷兰
bravely *adv.* 勇敢地

that made him so popular in his village may have come from being so *henpecked* in his house. After all, consider the men who are sweet, easy, and willing to please in the world; they are often those who are under the control of a sharp-tongued shrew at home. By causing this *sweetness* in her husband, a *shrewish* wife may in some ways be considered a *reasonable* blessing—and if so, Rip Van Winkle was thoroughly blessed.

It is certain that he was a great favorite among all the good wives of the village. They always took his side in family quarrels and lay all the blame on Dame Van Winkle. The children of the village, too, would shout with joy whenever he approached. He taught them

---

在村子里颇有好人缘，而这种温文尔雅又很可能源自他的惧内症。毕竟，想一想世上那些和蔼可亲的、随和的、讨人喜欢的男人是什么样，就什么都明白了。他们往往是在家里受一个伶牙俐齿的泼妇控制的人。只要能使丈夫甜蜜可爱，拥有一个泼辣的妻子，从某些方面来说，或许是一种福分呢！——假如真是这样的话，那么，李普·范·温克尔就是太有福分了。

可以肯定，他在全村的贤惠妻子中是最受宠的人。在他们夫妻吵架时，她们全都站在他这一边，全都责怪范·温克尔夫人。每当他一走近，村里的孩子们就会欢呼。他教他们做游戏，给他们制作玩具，还讲长长的

---

henpecked *adj.* 惧内的
shrewish *adj.* 脾气坏且爱争吵的

sweetness *n.* 令人愉快；讨人喜欢
reasonable *adj.* 合理的；公道的

games, made their playthings, and told them long stories of *ghosts* and *devils* and Indians. The children followed him all over the village, hanging on his coat and playing tricks on him. And not a dog would bark at him throughout the village.

The great *weakness* in Rip's character was a powerful dislike of all kinds of *profitable* work. This laziness could not be from a lack of patience or energy. He could sit on a wet rock and fish all day without a single complaint. He could carry a heavy gun on his shoulder for hours, walking through woods and up hills, to shoot a few rabbits or wild birds. He would never refuse to help a neighbor with the roughest work. And he was the best man for preparing

鬼怪故事和印第安人的故事。在村子里，他走到哪儿，孩子们就跟到哪儿，他们把他的衣服悬挂起来，还搞恶作剧。在整个村子里，就连狗也不会对他吠叫。

李普性格中最大的弱点是对所有有利可图的工作嗤之以鼻。他的懒惰不可能是由于缺少耐心或精力。他可以坐在一块湿漉漉的石头上钓鱼，一整天毫无怨言。他可以肩上扛着一杆沉重的猎枪，一连几个小时在树林里穿行或爬山，去猎获几只野兔或野鸟。他从不拒绝帮助邻居干最粗最脏的活。他是在所有乡村晚会上制作玉米食物的一流高手，最擅长修建石头篱

ghost *n.* 鬼；幽灵　　　　　devil *n.* 魔鬼
weakness *n.* 弱点　　　　　profitable *adj.* 有利可图的

Indian corn at all country parties, or for building stone *fences*, or for doing little jobs for the women of the village that their husbands wouldn't do. *In a word*, Rip was ready to pay attention to anybody's business but his own. To do his family duty or to keep his farm in order—he found these things impossible. His own poor farm—the falling-down fences, the wandering cow, the bare field—was the worst in the village. His son and daughter were poorly dressed and wild. They, and Rip's dog, Wolf, looked like they belonged to nobody.

Rip Van Winkle, however, was one of those happy men of *foolish*, easygoing natures who take the world lightly, eat white bread or brown, and would rather go hungry on a penny than work for a dollar. Alone, Rip would have whistled life away in perfect happiness. But

---

笆，最乐意为村里那些丈夫不干活的女人干零活。总之，李普的注意力随时准备用来管别人的事，唯独不管自己的事。要履行家庭的责任或把农场管理得井然有序之类的事，对他来说，根本就是不可能的。他那可怜的农场——倒塌的篱笆，四散的牛群，荒芜的田地——是村里最糟糕的农场。他的儿女是全村穿戴最破旧也是最缺少教养的野孩子。这些孩子，还有李普家叫"武夫"的狗看上去就像没有主人似的。

　　然而，李普·范·温克尔却属于这样一种幸福的人：他们天性愚蠢、懒散，对周围世界满不在乎，不管吃黑面包，还是吃白面包都无所谓，宁可因为没钱挨饿受冻也不为钱拼命干活。假如家里仅有他一个人的话，那

---

fence *n.* 栅栏　　　　　　　　　　　　　　　　　in a word 总之
foolish *adj.* 愚蠢的

his wife kept shouting in his ears about his *laziness*, his *carelessness*, and the ruin he was bringing on his family. Morning, noon, and night, her tongue was going non-stop. Everything Rip did produced a flood of shrewish talk. Rip's only reply to these angry speeches was to lift his *shoulders*, shake his head, roll his eyes, and go outside of the house—the only side which, in truth, belongs to the henpecked husband.

Times grew worse and worse with Rip Van Winkle as the years of *marriage* went by; a bitter heart never sweetens with age, and a tongue is the only edged tool that grows sharper with frequent use. Forced from home, Rip often found pleasure in a kind of club of wise men, philosophers, and other non-working men of the village.

么，他就会在完美的幸福中悠闲自在地打发人生，但他的妻子却不停地对着他的耳朵嚷嚷，说他懒惰、粗心，还说他把这个家给毁了。从早晨到中午，再到夜晚，她一直喋喋不休。李普所做的每一件事都会惹来一连串的数落。李普对这些气恼的话语所能做出的唯一反应就是耸耸肩，摇摇头，转转眼珠，然后走到屋外——说实话，这是他这个患有惧内症丈夫的唯一去处。

随着婚龄的增加，李普·范·温克尔的日子越来越难熬了；一颗苦涩的心不会因时光的流逝而变甜，而那带刃的舌剑却因频繁地使用而越发锋利。李普被逼无奈，经常在村里智者、哲人和那些闲人聚集的地方寻求

laziness *n.* 懒惰　　　　carelessness *n.* 粗心大意
shoulder *n.* 肩；肩膀　　marriage *n.* 结婚

They held their meetings under a great tree in front of the village *inn*, which travelers knew by its sign, a painted picture of King George the Third of England. Here the club's members used to sit in the shade through a long, lazy summer's day, talking of village matters, or telling endless, sleepy stories about nothing. Derrick Van Bummel, the well-dressed little *schoolmaster*, would sometimes read to them from an old newspaper. They would *discuss* with great seriousness events that had taken place some months before. These discussions were guided by the *innkeeper*, Nicholas Vedder, and his pipe. He never spoke a word, but when he disagreed with an opinion, black smoke came in quantity from the pipe, and when he agreed, he removed the pipe from his mouth and let the smoke curl sweetly about his nose.

---

欢乐。村里有个小旅店，游客一看见那个绘有英王乔治三世画像的招牌便知，旅店门前有一棵大树，他们就在树下聚会。这个小团体的成员常常在漫长而又闲散的夏日里整天坐在树阴下，谈论村里发生的大事小情或者讲述一些没完没了的、令人困倦的无关紧要的家长里短。德里克·范·巴麦尔是个衣着考究、身材瘦小的小学校长，他有时给他们朗读旧报纸。他们会表情严肃地讨论数月前发生的事件。这些讨论是在旅店老板尼古拉斯·威德和他的烟斗的指挥下进行的。他从来不发一言，但是，每当他反对一种意见时，他的烟斗里就会冒出大量的浓烟，他若赞同某种意见的话，就把烟斗从嘴里拿掉，让那烟从鼻孔里徐徐地绕出。

---

inn  *n.*  客栈；小旅馆　　　　　　　　　schoolmaster  *n.*  校长
discuss  *v.*  讨论　　　　　　　　　　　innkeeper  *n.*  客栈老板

Even from this *favorite* hiding place, however, Rip was chased by his wife. She would break in on the *peaceful* club meetings and direct her anger at all the club's members for *encouraging* laziness in her husband. In the end, poor Rip found only one way to escape the labor of the farm and the anger of Dame Van Winkle. This was to take gun in hand and walk away into the woods. He would sometimes sit at the foot of a tree and share his simple meal with Wolf, whom he saw as a fellow-sufferer. "Poor Wolf," he would say, "your lady leads you a dog's life; but never mind, my boy, while I live you will never lack a friend to stand by you!" The dog would *wag* his tail and look sadly in his master's face; and if dogs can feel pity, I do believe he returned the feeling with all his heart.

---

然而，即使在这个讨人喜欢的藏身之处，李普也还是被老婆追逐着。她会一下子冲进这个气氛和睦的会场向所有在场的人发泄不满，指责他们怂恿她丈夫懒惰。最终，可怜的李普发现要想逃避农活和范·温克尔夫人的愤怒只有一条路可走。那就是手握一杆猎枪走进树林。他有时会坐在一棵树下跟武夫分吃简单的食物，把这只狗当作自己的难友。"可怜的武夫"，他会说，"你的女主人让你过这种苦日子，但是，没关系，我的孩子，只要我活着，你身边就永远也不会缺少朋友！"听了这话，那狗就会摇摇尾巴，用悲哀的眼神看着主人的脸。假如狗能够感受到同情之心的话，我绝对相信这条狗会全心全意地回报这种感情。

---

favorite *adj.* 最喜爱的
encourage *v.* 鼓励

peaceful *adj.* 和平的
wag *v.* 摇；摆动（尾巴）

On one of these wanderings on a fine autumn day, Rip had unknowingly *climbed* to one of the highest parts of the Catskill mountains. He was hunting rabbits, and the *stillness* of the woodlands had echoed and re-echoed with the sound of his gun. Tired and out of breath, he threw himself, late in the afternoon, on a small round green hill covered with mountain bushes. From an opening between the trees he could overlook all the lower country with its miles of rich *woodland*. He saw at a distance the lordly Hudson River, far, far below him, moving on its silent but noble course. On the other side he looked down into a deep mountain *valley*, wild and lonely, the bottom filled with rocks that had fallen from the high hills above. Evening was approaching. The mountains began to throw their long blue shadows over the valleys. He saw that it would be dark before he could reach the village, and he sighed

---

　　在一个晴朗的秋日，李普又在这样游荡着，不知不觉地爬上了凯兹盖尔山脉的一处最高峰。他正在猎兔，寂静的林地不停地回荡着他的枪声。到了下午晚些时候，他已筋疲力尽、气喘吁吁，便在一座圆形的长满了灌木丛的绿色小山上躺下了。从树木间的空隙处，他可以俯瞰山下那有着绵延数英里富饶林带的整个乡村。他看到了在他下方，远处那高傲气派的哈德孙河正在静默而又庄严地流淌。在另一侧，他看到了一座深深的山谷，满目荒芜和孤寂，谷底布满了从高山上滚落的岩石。傍晚来临了。大山开始把它那长长的阴影投向深谷。他看出天黑之前他是到不了家了，而一想到还要面对范·温克尔夫人的暴怒，他就深深地叹了一口气。

---

climb *v.* 爬　　　　　　　　　　　　　　stillness *n.* 沉静
woodland *n.* 森林；林地　　　　　　　　valley *n.* 山谷

heavily when he thought of being met with the terrors of Dame Van Winkle.

As he was about to *descend*, he heard a voice from a distance, shouting, "Rip Van Winkle! Rip Van Winkle!" He looked round, but could see nothing but a blackbird flying its lonely way across the mountain. He thought his *imagination* must have tricked him, and turned again to descend, when he heard the same cry through the still evening air: "Rip Van Winkle! Rip Van Winkle!" Wolf made a low noise in his throat and drew nearer to his master's side, looking *fearfully* down the valley. Rip now felt a strong uncertainty coming over him. He looked *anxiously* in the same direction, and saw a strange figure working its way up the rocks, and bending under the weight of something he carried on his back. Rip was surprised to see any human being in this lonely place, but thinking it might be

---

　　就在他即将起身下山的时候，他听到远处传来一个声音，那声音在喊："李普·范·温克尔！李普·范·温克尔！"他环顾四周，除了一只孤零零的黑鸟正在飞跃大山以外，别的什么也没看见。他以为是出现了什么幻觉，便又转身朝下观望。这时，那声音又通过寂静的晚空传了过来："李普·范·温克尔！李普·范·温克尔！"武夫在喉咙里发出低低的吼声，而且越来越向主人靠近，惊恐地俯视着深谷。李普感到有一种奇怪的不安在向他袭来。他焦虑地望着同一方向，看到一个奇怪的人影正吃力地攀岩而上，背上背着的东西把腰都压弯了。在这种荒僻的地方居然能看到一个同类，李普感到非常吃惊，但一想到这人有可能是个村民，正需要他

---

descend　*v.*　下去；下降
fearfully　*adv.*　可怕地

imagination　*n.*　想象
anxiously　*adv.*　不安地；忧虑地

one of the villagers in need of his help, he hurried down to give it.

As he approached he was still more surprised by the stranger's *appearance*. He was a short square-built old fellow, with thick bushy hair and a beard. He was dressed in the old Dutch fashion—a short cloth coat belted at the waist, and broad trousers gathered at the *knees*. He carried on his back a heavy *barrel*, the kind that holds beer or whiskey, and he made signs for Rip to approach and help with his load. Though rather shy and *distrustful* of the stranger, Rip gave help with his usual speed. Helping each other, they climbed up the dry bed of a mountain stream. As they climbed, Rip heard long, deep rolling sounds, like distant thunder. The sound seemed to come out of an opening in the hill above them. He stopped briefly, but decided that it was only a mountain thunder-shower, and continued to climb.

---

的帮助，就赶紧走了过去。

走近一看，更加吃惊了，因为这个陌生人的外貌非常奇特。这是一位五短身材的老人，长着浓密的头发和胡须，衣着打扮完全是古老的荷兰样式——短短的布上衣，腰中束一条带子，宽大的裤子束拢于膝部。他背了一个很沉重的桶，是那种装啤酒或威士忌的桶，他示意李普过去帮他背桶。李普虽然有些害羞，对这个陌生人不太放心，但还是像往常一样痛快地过去帮忙。他们相互搀扶着爬上一条干涸的河床。在他们向上爬的时候，李普听到了什么东西发出的悠长而又低沉的滚动声，很像远处的雷声。那声音好像来自上方山头的一块空地。他驻足倾听，断定那不过是一

---

appearance *n.* 外貌；外观
barrel *n.* 桶

knee *n.* 膝盖
distrustful *adj.* 怀疑的

Passing through the opening in the hill, the two men came into a round open space, an *amphitheater*. It was *surrounded* by high hills with tall trees on their tops, so you could see little of the darkening sky or the bright evening cloud. During the whole time Rip and the stranger had climbed in silence. Although Rip wondered greatly at the purpose of carrying a barrel of strong drink up this wild mountain, there was something strange about the unknown that *kept* him *silent*.

On entering the amphitheater, he was greeted by still more *unusual* sights. On a level spot in the center was a company of odd-looking fellows playing at nine-pins, slowly rolling the balls at the wooden pins. Some of the men wore jackets, others wore short coats, with knives in their belts. Most of them wore broad trousers

种山里的雷雨声，于是，又接着往上爬。他们两个穿过山中的空地，来到一块圆形的空场，是个竞技场，周围环绕着高山，山顶古树参天，所以，几乎看不见那渐渐暗下来的天空，也看不见傍晚的白云。李普和陌生人在整个爬山过程中一直默默无语。尽管他对背着酒桶爬上这荒山野岭颇感纳闷，但由于不知道要发生什么事，这种奇怪的感觉使他保持缄默。

　　一到达竞技场，眼前的景象就更加奇特了。在竞技场中间一块平坦的地方有一伙相貌古怪的人在玩九柱戏，球在木柱之间慢慢地滚动。他们中有些人穿夹克衫，有些人穿运动衫，腰间的带子上都佩着刀，多数人都穿

amphitheater *n.* 竞技场　　　　surround *v.* 围绕；包围
keep silent 保持沉默　　　　unusual *adj.* 不寻常的

like Rip's guide. Their whole appearance was strange. One had a large head, broad face, and small piggish eyes. Another's face seemed to consist mostly of nose, and was topped by a pointed white hat with a red feather in it. There was one who seemed to be the *commander*. He was a fat old *gentleman*, with a weather-beaten face. He wore a formal black jacket, a broad belt and sword, red stockings, and high-heeled shoes with roses on them. The whole group reminded Rip of the figures in an old Dutch painting he had seen in the house of Dominic Van Shaick, the village *minister*, and which had been brought over from Holland when the colony was first settled.

What seemed especially odd to Rip was the way these folks played at their game of nine-pins. They kept the most serious faces

---

着像带李普来的那个人穿的那种宽松裤子。他们的容貌总体说来是很奇怪的。一个是大头、宽脸，睁着一双小小的，像猪一样的眼睛。另一个人的脸好像大部分都给鼻子占据了。他的头上戴着尖顶白帽子，上面插着红色的羽毛。有一个看上去是指挥官，是个胖胖的老绅士，有着一张饱经风霜的面孔。他穿着一件正统的黑色夹克衫，腰间系着一条宽带，上面佩着一把剑，脚穿一双红色的长袜，高跟鞋，上面还缀有玫瑰花。这伙人使李普想起了一幅古老的荷兰油画上的人物，那幅油画是他在村里的牧师多米尼克·范·塞克家里看到的，是在北美殖民地刚刚建立时从荷兰带过来的。

对李普来说尤为古怪的是这些人玩九柱戏的玩法。他们在玩时表情极为严肃，而且始终保持着极为神秘的沉默。唯一的声音就是球撞击木柱发

---

commander *n.* 指挥官　　　　　　　gentleman *n.* 先生；绅士
minister *n.* 牧师

as they played, and the most mysterious silence. The only sound was that of the balls hitting the wooden pins and echoing along the mountains like rolling thunder.

As Rip and his *companion* approached them, they suddenly stopped their play. They looked straight at him with such statue-like faces that his heart turned within him, and his knees knocked together. His companion now emptied the contents of the barrel into large drinking cups, and made signs for him to serve the company. He *obeyed*, shaking with fear. The men drank in the deepest silence, and then returned to their game.

*Gradually*, Rip's anxiety lessened. He even dared, when no eye was fixed upon him, to taste the drink, which he thought had much the flavor of a fine Holland whiskey. He was *naturally* a thirsty fellow,

出的声音和像滚雷隆隆地回荡于山间的回声。

　　当李普和他的同伴走近他们的时候，他们一下子停止了游戏，以雕像般的表情直盯盯地看着他，把他看得心都直翻个儿，双腿直绊架。这时，他的同伴开始把桶里的酒倒进一个个大酒杯里，示意他给那些人端过去。他虽然吓得浑身发抖，但还是照做了。那些人在极度的沉默中把酒喝干，然后又去接着玩游戏。

　　渐渐地，李普的紧张放松下来，在没有人看着他的时候，甚至还胆大地尝了尝他们的美酒，他觉得这酒跟一种荷兰威士忌的味道极为相似。他天生喜欢喝酒，所以，很快又斟了一杯。就这样，一会儿尝一杯，一会儿

companion *n.* 同伴；朋友
gradually *adv.* 逐步地；渐渐地

obey *v.* 服从；听从
naturally *adv.* 天生地；自然地

and soon allowed himself a second drink. One taste led to another, and he repeated his visits to the drinking cup so often that finally his senses were overpowered. His eyes swam in his head, his head gradually dropped to his *chest*, and he fell into a deep sleep.

When he awoke, he found himself on the small round green hill where he had first seen his companion, the old man of the valley. He *rubbed* his eyes—it was a bright sunny morning. The birds were jumping and singing in the bushes. "Surely," thought Rip, "I have not slept here all night?" He remembered what had happened before he fell asleep. The strange man with the barrel—the climb up the dry stream-bed—the amphitheater among the rocks—the strange serious party at nine-pins—the drinking cup. "Oh! That cup! That evil cup!" thought Rip. "What *excuse* shall I make to Dame Van Winkle?"

---

尝一杯，一杯接一杯，终于开始神志不清了。他头晕目眩，头渐渐地垂落胸前，进入了深深的睡眠状态。

一觉醒来，他发觉自己原来是睡在初次见到他的同伴，就是那个山谷老人时的那个圆形的绿色小山上。他揉了揉眼睛——天已经亮了，是个晴朗的早晨。鸟儿在树丛间欢快地雀跃鸣啭。李普心想："我肯定不是在这里睡了一夜吧？"他记起了睡觉前所发生的一切。那个身背酒桶的陌生人，沿着干涸的河床向上爬，岩石中的竞技场，玩九柱戏的那伙稀奇古怪的面无表情的人，还有酒杯。"噢！那酒杯！那邪恶的酒杯！"李普心想。"我得怎么向范·温克尔夫人交代呢？"

---

chest *n.* 胸；胸部

excuse *n.* 借口；理由

rub *v.* 擦

He looked round for his gun, but in place of the clean well-oiled *weapon*, he found an old gun, its iron time-worn and its wood worm-eaten. He now *suspected* that the serious games-players of the mountain had tricked him with strong drink and stolen his gun. Wolf, too, had disappeared, though he might have gone after rabbits or birds. He whistled for him and called his name, but no dog came.

He *decided* to revisit the scene of last night's events, and if he met with any of the group, to demand his gun and his dog. As he rose to walk, he felt an unusual tightness in his legs, arms, and all his body. "These mountain beds do not agree with me," thought Rip. He descended again into the deep valley. He found the dry stream-bed which he and his companion had climbed up the evening before.

---

他向四下里看了看，想找猎枪。然而，那把干净的、上好了油的猎枪不见了，取而代之的是一杆破枪，铁质部分锈迹斑斑，木质部分虫蛀腐朽。他开始怀疑山里那些玩九柱戏的表情严肃的人设计用烈酒把他灌醉，然后偷他的枪。武夫怎么也消失得无影无踪？不过，它也许是去追赶野兔或野鸟了。于是，他又是吹口哨，又是呼喊它的名字，可就是没有一条狗跑过来。

他决定再去昨晚发生一连串事件的地方看看，不管能遇上那伙人中的哪一个，都把枪和狗要回来。他正起身要走，突然，双腿、双臂，还有全身出现一阵不同寻常的紧巴巴的感觉。他想，"在山里睡觉毕竟是不适应啊。" 他又朝深谷走去，发现了他和他的同伴前一天晚上爬过的干涸

---

weapon  *n.*  武器；兵器
decide  *v.*  决定

suspect  *v.*  怀疑

But to his great surprise a mountain stream was now rushing down it, leaping from rock to rock and filling the valley with its pleasant sound. With difficulty he climbed up its sides, fighting his way through thick *bushes* and the branches of small trees.

Finally, he came to the place where an opening had led through the hill to the amphitheater; but no signs of such an opening remained. Only high rocks greeted him, and the stream that flowed quickly over them. Here, then, poor Rip was brought to a stop. He called again and whistled for his dog; he was answered only by the blackbirds flying high in the trees above him. What could he do? The morning was passing away, and he was very hungry. He *shook* his head, shouldered the old gun, and turned his steps toward home.

---

的河床。但是，令他大吃一惊的是，一条山溪正奔涌而泻，越过一块块岩石，整个山谷充满了悦耳的流水声。他艰难地沿着溪岸向上爬去，吃力地穿过浓密的树丛和小树的枝丫。

他终于来到了可以通往山中竞技场的地方，但那片空地已不复存在，呈现在他面前的只有高耸的岩石和那条从身边奔涌而过的溪流。没错，可怜的李普就是被那人带到这里的。他又开始唤狗，但回答他的只有那些在他上方的树间高高飞翔的黑鸟。该怎么办呢？整个上午就这样过去了，他饥肠辘辘。摇了摇头，扛起破枪，转身朝家走去。

---

bush *n.* 灌木　　　　　shake *v.* 摇（头）

As he approached the village, he met a number of people, but he knew none of them. This surprised him, for he had thought he knew everyone in the country around. Their clothes, too, were in a *fashion* different from the one he knew. They looked equally surprised to meet him. Many of them brought their hands to their *chins* when they saw him, and when Rip *copied* the movement he found, to his surprise, that his beard had grown a foot long!

He had now entered the village. A group of strange children ran at his *heels*, shouting after him and pointing at his long gray beard. The dogs barked as he passed. The village itself was changed; it was larger, with many more people. There were rows of houses he had never seen before. Strange names were over the doors—strange

---

　　快到村口的时候，他遇上了一伙人，但他一个也不认识。他感到吃惊，因为他一向觉得自己认识乡里乡亲中所有的人。他们的衣着打扮也与他所熟识的式样截然不同。那些人也同样吃惊地看着他。许多人看到他就伸手去摸脸颊，李普也模仿他们的动作，伸手摸摸脸颊，他惊讶地发现自己的胡须已经长了足有一英尺长！

　　终于进了村。一帮陌生的孩子跟在他后边跑，边跑边指着他长长的花白胡子喊。所有的狗都在他路过时对着他狂吠。村子也变了样，变大了，人也多多了，还盖起了一排排他以前从未见过的房屋。门上写着陌生的名

---

fashion　*n.*　（衣服）样式　　　　　　chin　*n.*　下巴
copy　*v.*　模仿；复制　　　　　　　　heel　*n.*　脚后跟

faces at the windows— everything was strange. He began to wonder whether some kind of magic was at work. Surely this was his own village, which he had left just the day before. There stood the Catskill mountains; there was the silver Hudson at a distance. Rip was very *confused*. "That cup last night," thought he, "has mixed up my brain thoroughly!"

It was with some difficulty that he found the way to his own house, which he approached with some fear, expecting every moment to hear the angry voice of Dame Van Winkle. But he found the house in *ruins*—the roof fallen in, the windows broken, the doors hanging off. He entered the house, which, to tell the truth, Dame Van Winkle had always kept in neat order. It was a sad, empty shell. Frightened, he called loudly for his wife and children. The lonely

---

字，窗前露出陌生的面孔，一切都是陌生的。他开始纳闷这里是不是被施了什么魔法。这里肯定是他自己的村子，不过是昨天才离开的。凯兹盖尔山峰依然在那里高高地耸立，银色的哈德孙河依然在远方奔流不息。李普真是困惑极了。他心里想："昨晚的那杯酒把脑袋全给搅糊涂了！"

他费了好大的劲才找到了回自家的路。他越是走近，就越是担心，觉得随时都可能听到范·温克尔夫人愤怒的吼声。然而，他却发现他的家已成废墟——屋顶塌陷，窗户破损，门在门框上悠荡着。他走进屋去。屋里，说实话，温克尔夫人一向收得井然有序，而现在，却成了一个可悲的空壳。他害怕了，高声呼唤老婆孩子。空屋子里一时间响起了他的声音，随后便又鸦雀无声了。

---

confused *adj.* 迷惑的          ruin *n.* 废墟

rooms rang for a moment with his voice, and then all again was silence.

He now hurried away toward his club's old meeting place at the village's small inn—but it too was gone. In its place stood a large *ugly* wooden building with the word HOTEL above the door. Instead of the great tree in front of it, there was a tall wooden pole, and from it hung a flag with a strange *pattern* of stars and stripes in red, white, and blue. He saw the inn's old sign, but even this was changed. King George's round face was the same, but his red coat was changed to one of blue. Instead of a crown, he wore a hat and held a *sword*. And underneath the picture, in large letters, was painted:

GENERAL WASHINGTON.

There was, as usual, a crowd of folk near the door, but no one

---

他又赶紧奔向村口小旅店他们那一伙人聚会的老地方——发现原来的一切也已不复存在，取而代之的是一座高大丑陋的木制建筑，门上书写着"旅馆"两个大字。前面的那棵大树变成了一根高大的木桩，上面挂着一面旗子，旗上有着奇怪的红、白、蓝相间的星条图案。他看到了小旅店的旧招牌，但就连这块招牌也变了样。乔治王的圆脸依旧，但他的红外衣变成了蓝外衣。他没有戴王冠，却戴了一顶帽子，还举着一把宝剑，头像下方有一些大写的字母：

GENERAL WASHINGTON（华盛顿将军）

门口，同以往一样，有一群人，但没有一个是李普记得的。他用月光

---

ugly *adj.* 丑陋的                                    pattern *n.* 图案
sword *n.* 剑；刀

that Rip remembered. He looked for wise old Nicholas Vedder with his *pipe*, or the little schoolmaster Van Bummel, reading from an old newspaper. In place of these men, a thin, nervous-looking fellow was shouting a speech to the crowd about *government—freedom—citizens—elections—heroes* of the revolutionary war—and other words completely unknown to the confused Van Winkle.

The appearance of Rip, with his long beard, old gun, strange clothes, and an army of women and children at his heels, attracted the attention of the politicians in the crowd. They gathered round him, eyeing him from head to foot with great curiosity. The thin speech-maker hurried up to him, and bringing him to one side, asked "on which side he *voted*?" Rip looked at him with complete, empty stupidity. "I say, which political party do you belong to?"

搜寻着那位富有智慧的、总是叼着烟斗的老尼古拉斯·威德，或者是身材瘦小的、总是给大家读旧报纸的小学校长范·巴麦尔。这些人都不见了，见到的是一个清瘦的、表情紧张的人，他正对着人群高声演讲，讲什么政府——自由——公民——选举——革命战争的英雄们——还有其他一些对困惑的范·温克尔来说全然不知的字眼。

　　李普的出现，还有他的长须、破枪、奇怪的服装以及身后跟着的一大群妇女和儿童，吸引了人群中那些搞政治的人的注意力。他们聚拢过来，以极大的好奇心上下打量着他。那个清瘦的演讲者冲到他面前，把他拉到一边，问："你投哪一方的票？"李普脑海里一片茫然，傻乎乎地看着他。"我说，你属于哪一个政党？"那人又问。李普不知道该怎样回答

pipe *n.* 烟斗　　　　　　　　　　　government *n.* 政府
freedom *n.* 自由　　　　　　　　　　vote *v.* 投票；选举

the man insisted. Rip had no idea how to answer such a question. Then a knowing, self-important gentleman made his way through the crowd, putting folks to the right and left with his *elbows* as he passed. He positioned himself before Van Winkle, and demanded in a serious voice "what brought him to the *election* with a gun on his shoulder and a wild crowd at his heels, and whether he meant to cause trouble in the village?"—"Oh, dear, gentlemen," cried Rip, "I am a poor quiet man, a native of the place, and a faithful subject of the king, God bless him!"

Here a general shout burst from the bystanders: "A *spy*! a spy! the enemy! away with him!" It was with great difficulty that the self-important man brought order again to the crowd. Then, with even deeper *seriousness* than before, he demanded of the stranger why

---

这个问题。这时，一位世故的、妄自尊大的绅士从人群中挤过来，边挤边用胳膊肘把人左右推开。他在范·温克尔面前摆好架势，厉声询问是什么使他肩扛猎枪，还带着一大群疯狂的人来参加选举，是不是想在村子里捣乱。"噢，天哪，先生，"李普嚷道，"我是一个安分守己的人，在这里土生土长，是国王忠实的臣民。上帝保佑吾王！"

这时，围观的人们一致高喊："间谍！间谍！敌人！把他赶走！"妄自尊大的家伙费了好大力气才重新整理好人群的秩序。接着，以更严肃的口气要求这个陌生人回答为什么到这儿来，是来找谁的。我们这位可怜的

---

elbow *n.* 肘部
spy *n.* 间谍

election *n.* 选举
seriousness *n.* 严肃；认真

he had come there, and whom he was searching for? The poor man promised that he meant no harm, but merely came in search of some of his neighbors, who used to meet at the old hotel.

"Well—who are they?—name them."

Rip thought for a moment, then asked, "Where's Nicholas Vedder?"

There was a silence for a while, then an old man replied, in a thin little voice, "Nicholas Vedder! Why, he is dead and gone these eighteen years! There was a *wooden* marker in the *churchyard* that used to tell about him, but that's rotten and gone, too."

"Where's Van Bummel, the schoolmaster?"

"Oh, he went off to the army, right at the beginning of the war. He became a famous *general*, and now he's in the government."

---

人保证说绝无害人之心，只不过是来找几个邻居，这些人过去常在老旅店这儿会面。

"那好吧，说说看，他们是谁？"

李普想了一会儿，然后问道："尼古拉斯·威德在哪儿？"

人们一时间沉默无语，接着，一位老人用一种细微的声音回答说："尼古拉斯·威德！嗯，他已经死了十八年了！他的墓地里有一个木制的墓碑，上面对他作了介绍，可是，那个墓碑现在也已经烂掉了。"

"范·巴麦尔在哪儿？就是那位小学校长？"

"噢，他参了军，就在刚打仗的时候。他成了一位著名的将领，正在政府里做事呢。"

---

wooden *adj.* 木制的                              churchyard *n.* 墓地
general *n.* 将军；上将

Rip's heart died away at hearing of these sad changes in his home and friends, and finding himself so alone in the world. Every answer *puzzled* him, too, by mentioning matters he could not understand—eighteen years, and war, and *revolution*, and government. So when the self-important man finally asked him who he was, he cried out, "God knows! I'm not myself —I'm somebody else—I was myself last night, but I fell asleep on the mountain, and they've changed my gun, and everything's changed, and I'm changed, and I can't tell what's my name or who I am!"

The by-standers began now to look at each other, give little smiles, close one eye, and press their fingers against their foreheads. At this very moment, a pretty young woman passed through the *crowd* to have a look at the gray-bearded man. She had a round little

---

知道了有关家里和朋友们这些令人悲哀的变化，发觉自己在这个世界上如此孤独，李普心灰意冷。人们提到的什么十八年啦，战争啦，革命啦，还有政府啦，等等，所有这些也都让他感到困惑。所以，当那位妄自尊大的家伙最后问起他是谁的时候，他就哭了起来。"天知道！我不是我自己了——我是别的什么人了——昨天晚上我还是我自己，但在山上睡着了，他们就把我的枪给换了，而且，一切都变了，连我自己也变了。我说不出我叫什么名字，也不知道我是谁！"

围观的人们开始你看看我，我看看你，都不笑了，有的还闭上一只眼，把手压在额头上。就在这时，一位年轻漂亮的女人从人群中穿过来，打量着这位有着花白胡子的老人。她怀里抱着 个胖胖的小孩，那孩子一

---

puzzle  *v.*  迷惑；使困惑  
crowd  *n.*  人群；观众

revolution  *n.*  革命

child in her arms who, frightened by the strange old man, began to cry. "Hush, Rip," cried she, "hush, you little fool; the old man won't hurt you." The name of the child, the look of the mother, something in her voice, all awakened *memories* in his mind. "What is your name, my good woman?" asked he.

"Judith Gardenier."

"And your father's name?"

"Ah, *poor* man, Rip Van Winkle was his name, but it's twenty years since he went away from home with his gun, and never has been heard of since. His dog came home without him; but whether he

见这陌生的老头就吓哭了。"别哭，李普，"她大声哄着孩子。"别哭，你这小傻瓜，老头不会伤害你。"孩子的名字，母亲的相貌，还有母亲声音里的某种东西，一下子唤起了他脑海中的记忆。"你叫什么名字，可爱的夫人？"他问。

"朱迪斯·加德纳。"

"你父亲叫什么名字？"

"噢，我可怜的父亲，他叫李普·范·温克尔，可是他带着猎枪离家出走已经有二十年了，始终没有一点儿消息。他的狗是自己跑回来的，可他到

memory *n.* 记忆　　　　　　　　　　　　poor *adj.* 可怜的

shot himself or was carried away by *Indians*, nobody can tell. I was only a little girl then."

Rip had only one more question to ask; but he said with a shaking voice: "Where's your mother?"

"Oh, she too died, just a short time ago. She had a heart *attack* while shouting at a traveling *salesman*."

There was some comfort, at least, in this information. The honest man could no longer control himself. He gathered his daughter and her child in his arms. "I am your father!" he cried. "Young Rip Van Winkle once; old Rip Van Winkle now! Does nobody know poor Rip

---

底是自杀了，还是让印第安人给掠走了，没有人知道。我那时还小。"

李普现在只有一个问题了，他声音颤抖地问："你妈妈在哪儿？"

"噢，她也死了，刚死不久。她是对一个推销员嚷嚷时心脏病猝发而死的。"

这个消息，对李普来说，至少也是个安慰。这个老实人再也控制不住了，他一把搂过女儿和她怀里的孩子，哭着说："我就是你的父亲！我曾经是年轻的李普·范·温克尔，现在是老李普·范·温克尔！没人认识李

---

Indian *n.* 印第安人
salesman *n.* 推销员

attack *n.* （疾病）发作；攻击

Van Winkle?"

All stood in silent wonder, until an old woman came out of the crowd, looked closely at his face for a moment, and finally cried, "Sure enough! It is Rip Van Winkle! It is himself! Welcome home again, old neighbor. Why, where have you been these twenty long years?!"

Rip's story was soon told, for the entire twenty years had been to him just as one night. The neighbors at first could not believe it. They *shook* their heads in doubt, and smiled their smiles at *each other*. However, they decided to get the *opinion* of old Peter Vanderdonk, who was seen then slowly advancing up the road. He was descended from the famous *historian* of that name, who wrote

---

普·范·温克尔吗？"

　　大家全都惊奇地呆立着，一直到有个老太太从人群中走出来，对着他的面孔仔细端详了好一会儿，最后大声说："一点儿没错！是李普·范·温克尔！真是他本人！我的老邻居，你可回来了。二十年了，你跑到哪儿去了？！"

　　李普的事儿很快就传开了，因为整整二十年对他来说就是短短的一夜。起初，邻居们不相信，都怀疑地摇头，相视一笑。然而，他们还是决定听听老彼得·范德丹克的意见，有人看见他正缓缓地从公路那边走来。他是著名历史学家范德丹克的后裔。这位历史学家著有一部最早的本地区

---

shake *v.* 摇动；抖动
opinion *n.* 意见；主张

each other 彼此；互相
historian *n.* 历史学家

one of the earliest accounts of the *region*. Peter was the oldest man in the village, and very *knowledgeable* about all the wonderful events and *traditions* of the neighborhood. He remembered Rip immediately, and supported his story in the most *satisfactory* manner. He stated as a historical fact that the Catskill tains had always had magical qualities. There was no doubt, he said, that the great Hendrick Hudson, the first discoverer of the river and country, returned every twenty years with the crew of his ship. In this way, Hudson could revisit the scene of his adventures and keep a guardian eye on the river. Vanderdonk's own father had once seen them in their old Dutch clothes playing at nine-pins in a valley of the mountains. And he himself had heard, one summer afternoon, the sound of their balls,

---

地方志。彼得是村里年龄最长的老人，他对附近一带惊人的事件和传统颇有学问。他马上就记起了李普，而且以最令人满意的方式为李普的故事提供了确凿的证据。他声明凯兹盖尔山脉一向具有神奇的特质，认为这是一个历史事实。毫无疑问，他说，了不起的亨德里克·哈德逊，就是第一位发现哈德逊河及这片区域的人，每二十年就带着船员一起回来一次。这样，哈德逊就可以重访他的探险地而且还能密切关注哈德逊河。范德丹克的父亲就曾亲眼见过他们身穿古老的荷兰服装在一个山谷里玩九柱戏。他本人也在一个夏日的下午听到过他们滚球的隆隆声，很像远处的滚雷。

---

region *n.* 地区；范围
tradition *n.* 惯例；传统

knowledgeable *adj.* 知识渊博的
satisfactory *adj.* 令人满意的

like distant rolling thunder.

To make a long story short, the company broke up, and returned to the more important matters of the election. Rip's daughter took him home to live with her. And in time, Rip again began his old walks and *habits*. He soon found many of his old friends, all of them rather the worse for the wear and tear of time. He preferred the younger people of the village, who grew to like him, too. He could often be found sitting in his old place outside the hotel.

It was some time before he could understand the strange *events* that had taken place during his sleep: There had been a revolutionary war; the country was no longer a *prisoner* of old England; and, instead of being a subject of King George the Third of England, he was now a free *citizen* of the United States of America.

---

长话短说，围观的人们终于散了，他们又去忙于更重要的有关选举方面的事情了。李普的女儿把老父亲带回家跟自己一起生活。李普呢，马上就故态复萌，他的生活方式、习惯还都是老一套。他很快就找到了许多老朋友，他们都已到了风烛残年，个个老弱不堪。他更喜欢跟村子里年纪轻些的人交往，他们也开始喜欢起他来。人们发现他经常在旅馆外面的老地方坐着。

过了相当一段时间他才弄明白在长眠的那段时间里所发生的各种奇怪事件：这里经历了革命战争，这个国家已不再受英国的控制；他已不再是英王乔治三世的臣民，而是美利坚合众国的自由公民。事实上，李普不是

---

habit *n.* 习惯；习性　　　　　　　　　　event *n.* 事件；大事
prisoner *n.* 囚犯；犯人　　　　　　　　citizen *n.* 公民

Rip, in fact, was no *politician*. The changes of states and government *leaders* made little impression on him. To be sure, he understood and was grateful for his freedom—from Dame Van Winkle. Whenever her name was mentioned, however, he only lifted his shoulders, shook his head, and rolled his eyes.

He used to tell his story to every stranger that arrived at the hotel. Some always doubted the reality of it, and insisted that Rip had been out of his head. But nearly all of the old Dutch villagers believed it fully. Even to this day, when they hear a *thunderstorm* on a summer afternoon in the Catskills, they say that Hendrick Hudson and his crew are at their game of nine-pins. And it is a common wish of all henpecked husbands in the neighborhood, when life hangs heavy on their hands, that they might have a quieting drink out of Rip Van Winkle's cup.

---

一个喜欢参政的人。国家和政府领导人的更换并没有给他留下什么印象。不过，可以肯定，他对自己摆脱了范·温克尔夫人的束缚这件事还是完全弄懂了，而且感到非常欣慰。然而，每当提起她的名字，他只是耸耸肩，摇摇头，转转眼珠。

不管是哪个生人来住店，他总是要给人家讲他的故事。有些人总怀疑这个故事的真实性，坚持认为李普头脑不正常。但是，几乎所有古老的荷兰村里的村民都对此深信无疑。即使到了今天，每当在夏日的午后听到凯兹盖尔山脉有雷雨声时，他们还会说亨德里克·哈德逊和他的船员们正在玩九柱戏。而且，附近一带凡是怕老婆的男人只要感到日子难熬了，就很希望能安静地喝上一杯李普·范·温克尔酒杯里的酒，这是他们的共同心愿。

---

politician  *n.* 从政者；政治家　　　　　　　　　　leader  *n.* 领导者
thunderstorm  *n.* 雷暴；雷雨交加

# The Journey to Hanford

Adapted from the story by William Saroyan

William Saroyan's family came to the United States from Armenia. His older brother and sisters were born there, and William was born in Fresno, California, in 1908. The Saroyan family was large and loving, but very poor. After Saroyan's father died when Saroyan was only three, his mother had no money at all. She had to put her children in an *orphanage* (a home for children with no parents) for five years. Saroyan began working at the age of eight, selling newspapers. He left school at the age of fourteen.

## 汉福德之行

根据威廉·萨罗扬的同名故事改写

威廉·萨罗扬一家是从亚美尼亚来到美国的。他的哥哥姐姐均出生于亚美尼亚，而威廉则于1908年出生在加州的弗雷斯诺。萨罗扬一家人口众多，相亲相爱，但很贫穷。他年仅三岁时，父亲就去世了。母亲身无分文，只得把孩子们送到孤儿院（失去双亲的儿童收养所）寄养了五年。他八岁开始工作——卖报，十四岁辍学。他决定要当一名作家，就通过读书来自学。他写过小说、诗歌和剧本。他的作品常常描写自

orphanage  *n.* 孤儿院

He decided to become a writer, and taught himself by reading. He wrote stories, *poems*, and *plays*. His work is often about his own life and his own family. The story that follows, "*A Journey to Hanford*" is from the book *My Name Is Aram*. All the stories in this book are told by Aram, a boy in a large, poor Armenian family in the California farmlands. Saroyan writes about the goodness of people and the richness of life. He often writes about how people are able to find happiness, hope, and joy in very difficult times. Saroyan himself was not always happy with life in the United States. After 1958, he lived mostly in Paris. But he kept his home in Fresno, and he died there in 1981.

I

The time came one year for my sad uncle Jorgi to get on his

---

己的生活和家庭。下面的文章"汉福德之行"节选自《我叫阿拉姆》一书。书中所有的故事都由阿拉姆讲述。阿拉姆是加州农村一户亚美尼亚移民的孩子，家里人口多，生活很贫穷。萨罗扬讴歌人性的善良，赞美生活的丰饶。他经常描写人们如何在极为艰难时期找到幸福、希望和欢乐。但他本人在美国的生活并不总是那么如意。1958年后，他多半生活在巴黎，但在弗雷斯诺的家也一直保留着。1981年，萨罗扬正是在那里与世长辞。

I

那　年，我那忧伤的叔叔乔奇终于要骑二十七英里路的自行车去汉福

poem　*n.*　诗歌　　　　　　　　　play　*n.*　剧本

bicycle and ride twenty-seven miles to Hanford. There was a job for him there in a farmer's field. Of course, before he went, the family had to decide who would go with him.

It is true that Jorgi was a kind of fool. That was all right with the family most of the time. But right now, in the summer, they wanted to forget him for a while. Now he would go away to Hanford and work in the watermelon fields. All would be well. He would earn a little money and at the same time be out of the way. That was the *important* thing—to get him out of the way.

"Away with him and his *zither* both," my grandfather said. "You will read in a book that a man can sit all day under a tree and play music on a zither and sing. Believe me, that writer is a fool. Money,

---

德了。有个农场主的地里有份活儿要他干。当然，在临走前，全家得决定谁和他一起去。

的确，乔奇有点儿傻，但一般情况下和家里人在一起还说得过去。可眼下，正值夏季，他们却要忽略他一阵儿。现在，他要去汉福德的西瓜地里干活了。一切都会如愿。他能挣点儿钱，同时也碍不着别人的事了。让他别碍事——那才是问题的关键。

"让他带上齐特琴一块儿走，"我祖父说。"你看书里写的，一个人整天坐在树底下弹齐特琴唱歌儿。说真的，那个写书的人就是个傻子。

---

important *adj.* 重要的　　　　　　　　　　　zither *n.* 齐特琴

that's the thing. Let him go and work under the sun for a while. In the watermelons. Him and his zither both."

"You say that now," my grandmother said, "but wait a week. Wait, and you will need music again."

"Foolish words!" my grandfather said. "You will read in a book that a man who sings is truly a happy man. But that writer is a dreamer, not a businessman in a thousand years. Let him go. It is twenty-seven miles to Hanford. That is a very good *distance*."

"You speak that way now," my grandmother said. "But in three days you will be a sad man. I will see you walking around like a tiger. I will see you *roar* with anger. I am the one who will see that. Seeing that, I am the one who will laugh."

---

钱，那才是真格的。让他到烈日底下干上一段时间，带上齐特琴一块儿去西瓜地"

"你现在这么说，"我祖母说，"可是，过一个星期再看，你又该要听他的音乐了。"

"说蠢话！"祖父说。"你看书里写的，唱歌的人是真正快乐的人。可那个写书的纯粹是在做梦，一千年也成不了商人。让他走。到汉福德有二十七英里的路，正经挺远呢。"

"你也就只能现在这么说，"祖母说。"不出三天你就得难受了。到时候看，你就得像个老虎似的到处转悠，气得干吼。别人不知道，我可是能看到。到那时，可别怪我笑话你。"

---

distance *n.* 距离  roar *v.* 吼叫

"You are a woman," said my grandfather. "You will read in a book that a woman is a perfect and beautiful thing. Believe me, that writer is not looking at his wife. He is dreaming."

"It is just that you are no longer young," my grandmother said. "That is why you are roaring."

"Close your mouth," my grandfather roared. "Close it right now!"

My grandfather looked around the room at his children and *grandchildren*. "I say he goes to Hanford on his bicycle," he said. "What do you say?"

Nobody spoke.

"Then it is done," my grandfather said. "Now, who shall we send with him on this journey? Which of our children shall we *punish* by

---

"你是个妇道人家，"祖父说，"书里说女人完美、漂亮。说真的，那个写书的没看看他自己的老婆什么样，纯粹是在做梦。"

"这是因为你不再年轻了，"祖母说。"怪不得你总是大吵大嚷的。"

"闭嘴，"祖父吼道。"赶紧闭嘴！"

祖父挨个儿看看屋里的子孙们，说："我说让他骑自行车去汉福德。你们说呢？"

没人吱声。

"那就这么定了，"祖父说。"现在说说看，该让谁陪他上路？该罚

---

grandchildren *n.* 孙子；孙女

punish *v.* 惩罚

sending him with Jorgi to Hanford? You will read in a book that a journey to a new city is a great thing for a young man. That writer is probably a fool of eighty or ninety. His only *journey* was two miles from home once when he was a little child. Who shall we punish? Vask? Shall Vask be the one? Step up here, boy."

My cousin Vask got up from the floor and stood in front of the old man. My grandfather put his hand over Vask's face. His hand almost *covered* the whole head.

"Shall you go with your uncle Jorgi to Hanford?" my grandfather said.

"If it pleases my grandfather, I will," Vask said.

---

哪个孩子，让他跟乔奇一起去汉福德？书里说，到一个新城市去旅行对年轻人来说是件很棒的事儿。那个写书的八成儿是个八九十岁的老傻瓜，没出过远门。就出去过一次，还是在小时候，刚走出去二里地，马上就回来了。该罚谁呢？瓦斯克？是不是该罚瓦斯克呢？瓦斯克，到这儿来。"

我堂弟瓦斯克从地板上站起来，走到老头儿面前。祖父用手摸摸他的脸，他的大手差不多把他整个脑袋都盖住了。

"你想和乔奇叔叔一起去汉福德吗？"祖父问。

"如果能让爷爷高兴的话，我就去。"瓦斯克说。

---

journey  n.  旅行

cover  v.  盖；盖住

The old man began to make faces, thinking about it.

"Let me think a minute," he said. "Jorgi is one of the *foolish* ones in our family. Vask is another. Is it wise to put two fools together? Let me hear your spoken thoughts on this."

"I think it is the right thing to do," my uncle Zorab said. "A fool and a fool. One to work, the other to clean house and cook."

"*Perhaps*," my grandfather said. "Can you cook, boy?"

"Of course he can cook," my grandmother said. "Rice, at least."

"Let the boy speak for himself," my grandfather said. "Is that true, boy, about the rice? Four cups of water, one cup of rice, a little

---

老头儿开始做鬼脸，考虑这件事。

"让我想想，"他说。"乔奇是咱们家的一个傻孩子，瓦斯克是另一个。把两个傻孩子放到一起是明智的做法吗？我想听听你们对这件事儿的想法。"

"我认为这么做很明智，"我叔叔左拉伯说。"傻子跟傻子在一起。一个干活，另一个收拾屋子、做饭。"

"或许吧，"我祖父说。"你会做饭吗，孩子？"

"他当然会做，"祖母说，"起码会焖饭。"

"让孩子自己说，"祖父说。"真的吗？孩子，会焖饭？四杯水，一

---

foolish  *adj.* 愚蠢的；傻的                                        perhaps  *adv.* 或许

*spoon* of salt. Do you know how to make it taste like food, and not *swill*, or am I dreaming?"

"I have cooked rice," Vask said. "It tasted like food. But it was salty. We had to drink water all day and all night."

"All right. It was salty," my grandfather said. "Of course you had to drink water all day and all night. We've all eaten rice like that." He turned to the others. He began to make faces again. "I think this is the boy to go," he said.

"On second thought," my uncle Zorab said, "two fools, one after the other, perhaps not. We have Aram here. I think he should go. Without question, he needs to be punished."

---

杯米，一小勺盐。你知道怎么才能让它吃起来像饭，而不像猪食吗？要么就是我在做梦？"

"我焖过米饭，"瓦斯克说。"吃着像饭，就是有点咸，得整天整夜地喝水。"

"不错，就是咸。"祖父说。"你们当然得整天整夜地喝水。咱们都是吃这样的饭。"他把脸转向大家，又开始做怪相，说："我看这个孩子去正合适。"

"再好好想想，"左拉伯叔叔说："两个傻瓜，一个跟着另一个，恐怕不行。还有阿拉姆呢，我认为他应该去。毫无疑问，他该受罚。"

---

spoon  *n.*  勺；匙　　　　　　　　　　　　swill  *n.*  泔水；猪食

Everyone looked at me.

"Aram?" my grandfather said. "You mean the boy who *laughs*? You mean loud-laughing Aram Garoghlanian? What has the boy done to be punished like this?"

"He knows," my uncle Zorab said.

My grandfather looked at me. "What have you done, boy?"

I knew he was not angry with me. I began to laugh, *remembering* the things I had done. My grandfather listened for a minute, then began laughing with me. We were the only Garoghlanians in the world who laughed that way.

"Aram Garoghlanian," he said. "I say again: What have you

---

所有人都把目光投向我。

"阿拉姆？"祖父说："你是说那个爱笑的孩子？就是总爱哈哈大笑的阿拉姆·加龙菲安尼亚？他干什么了，得这么罚他？"

"他自己知道，"左拉伯叔叔说。

祖父看着我，问："你干什么了，孩子？"

我知道他没生我的气。想起我做过的那些事，我又忍不住哈哈大笑。祖父听了一会儿，接着，就和我一起哈哈大笑起来。我们加龙菲安尼亚家族是世上唯一这样大笑的人。

"阿拉姆·加龙菲安尼亚，"他说。"我再问一遍：你都干了些什

---

laugh  *v.* 笑　　　　　　　　　　　　remember  *v.* 记得；记起

done?"

"Which one?" I said.

"You know which one," my uncle Zorab said.

"Do you mean," I said, "telling all our friends that you are out of your mind?"

My uncle Zorab said nothing.

"Or do you mean," I said, "going around talking the way you talk?"

"This is the boy to send with Jorgi," uncle Zorab said.

"Can you *cook* rice?" my grandfather said.

I understood *perfectly* now. If I could cook rice, I could go with

---

么？"

"哪一回？"我说。

"你知道是哪一回。"左拉伯叔叔说。

我问："你是指我告诉所有的朋友你把魂儿丢了那回吗？"

左拉伯叔叔不做声。

"还是说，到处转悠学你说话那回？"

"就该派这小子跟乔奇一块儿去，"左拉伯叔叔说。

"你会做饭吗？"祖父问。

现在我心里十分清楚。如果会做，就能和乔奇一块儿去汉福德。我可

---

cook  *v.* 煮；烹调                    perfectly  *adv.* 完全地

Jorgi to Hanford. I forgot about the writer who said a journey was a great thing. Fool or old or anything else, I wanted to go.

"I can cook rice," I said.

"Salty or swill, or what?" my grandfather said.

"Sometimes salty," I said. "Sometimes swill. Sometimes perfect."

"Let us think about this," my grandfather said. "Sometimes salty. Sometimes swill. *Sometimes* perfect. Is this the boy to send to Hanford?"

"Yes," my uncle Zorab said. "The only one."

"Then it is done," my grandfather said. "That will be all. I wish to be *alone*."

---

不管是哪个作家说过旅行是件新鲜事。我可不管他是傻瓜，是老头儿，还是别的什么，反正我就是想去。

"我会做饭。"我回答。

"咸的？像猪食的？还是像别的什么？"

我说："有时候咸，有时候像猪食，有时好吃极了。"

"咱们都想想，"祖父说。"有时候咸，有时候像猪食，有时候好吃极了。""这样的孩子是不是应该送到汉福德？"

"应该"，左拉伯叔叔说。"就应该送他。"

"那就这么定了，"祖父说。"行了，没事了，你们都走吧。"

---

sometimes  *adv.* 有时                                          alone  *adj.* 独自的；单独的

I started to go. My grandfather took me by the neck. "Stay a minute," he said. When we were alone, he said, "Talk the way your uncle Zorab talks."

I did, and my grandfather roared with *laughter*. "Go to Hanford," he said. "Go with the fool Jorgi and make it salty or make it swill or make it perfect."

II

We left the *following* morning before the sun was up. Sometimes Jorgi rode the bicycle and I walked, and sometimes I rode and Jorgi walked. We got to Hanford in the late afternoon.

The idea was for us to stay until Jorgi's job ended. So we looked around town for a house to live in. We found one that Jorgi liked

我正要走，祖父一把抓住我的脖子，说："等会儿。"待其他人都走后，他说："你左拉伯叔叔怎么说话，给我学学看。"

我就学了起来，把祖父逗得哈哈大笑，笑声震耳。"去汉福德吧，"他说。"和傻瓜乔奇一起去，给他做饭。做咸了，或做成猪食，或做得好吃极了，都随你的便。"

II

第二天一早，太阳还没出来，我们就出发了。有时，乔奇骑自行车，我徒步；有时我骑自行车，他徒步。天黑之前，我们到了汉福德。

我们要在这里呆到乔奇干完活，所以，就在镇里四处打听，想找个房

laughter *n.* 笑声　　　　　　following *adj.* （时间上）接着的

and moved in that night. The house had eleven rooms, running water, and a kitchen. One room had two beds in it, and all the other rooms were empty. After we moved in, Jorgi took out his zither, sat on the floor, and began to play and sing. It was beautiful. It was sad sometimes and sometimes funny, but it was always beautiful. I don't know how long he played, but *suddenly* he got up off the floor and said, "Aram, I want rice."

I made rice that night that was both salty and swill, but my uncle Jorgi said, "Aram, this is *wonderful*."

The birds got us up with the sun.

"The job," I said. "You begin today, you know."

"Today," my uncle Jorgi said in a *low*, sad voice.

---

子住下来。最后总算找到了乔奇喜欢的房子，当晚就住进去了。这个房子有十一个房间，有自来水，还有一个厨房。其中一个房间里有两张床，其他房间都是空的。我们刚搬进去，乔奇就拿出齐特琴，往门口一坐，开始边弹边唱。真好听！乐曲时而哀伤时而欢快，但从始至终都很优美。不知弹了多久，他突然站起来说，"阿拉姆，我想吃米饭。"

那天晚上我做的米饭又咸又像猪食，然而乔奇叔叔却说："阿拉姆，这饭真香。"

鸟儿叽喳地叫着，把我们吵醒了，太阳一出来，我们就起床了。

"那个活儿，"我说，"你今天就得干了。"

"今天就得干了。"乔奇叔叔很不痛快地低声说。

---

suddenly *adv.* 突然地          wonderful *adj.* 极好的；绝妙的
low *adj.* 低的

He walked slowly out of the empty house. I looked around for something to clean with, but found nothing. So I went out and sat on the *steps* to the *front* door. It seemed to be a nice part of the world in *daylight*. It was a street with only four houses. There was a church across the street from one of the houses. I sat on the steps for about an hour. My uncle Jorgi came up the street on his bicycle. The bicycle was going all over the place, and my uncle Jorgi was laughing and singing.

"Not this year, thank God," he said. He fell off the bicycle into a large plant covered with flowers.

"What?" I said.

"There is no job," he said. "No job, thank God."

---

他慢腾腾地走出了那空空的房子。我四处寻找打扫房间的工具，可是什么也没找到，就走出去坐在通往前门的台阶上。在阳光下，这个地方看起来还不错。这条街上只有四座房子，其中一个房子的对面是座教堂。我在台阶上坐了约一个小时，就见乔奇叔叔骑着车从街上回来了。他骑着车子，又是唱，又是笑，把这个地方逛了个遍。

"今年不行啦，感谢上帝，"他说。随即从车子上下来，跌进一大簇开满鲜花的植物丛里。

"什么？"我问。

"没有活儿，"他说。"没有活儿，感谢上帝。"

---

step *n.* 台阶
daylight *n.* 日光

front *adj.* 前面的

He *smelled* a flower.

"No job?" I said.

"No job, praise our Father above us."

"Why not?" I said.

"The watermelons," he said.

"What about them?" I said.

"The *season* is over," he said.

"That isn't true," I said.

"The season is over," my uncle Jorgi said. "*Believe* me, it is finished. Praise God, the watermelons are all gone. They have all been taken up."

"Who said so?" I said.

---

他凑近一朵花，闻了闻。
"没有活儿？"我问。
"没活儿，赞美我们的圣父吧。"
"为什么没有？"我问。
"那些西瓜，"他说。
"西瓜怎么了？"我问。
"过季了，"他说。
"不可能，"我说。
"过季了，"乔奇叔叔说。"真的，都罢园了。赞美上帝吧，西瓜都没了，都摘完了。"
"是谁说的？"我问。

---

smell  *v.*  闻；嗅                                      season  *n.*  季节
believe  *v.*  相信

"The farmer himself. The farmer himself said so," my uncle Jorgi said.

"He just said that," I said. "He didn't want to hurt you. He just said that because he knew your heart wouldn't be in your work."

"*Praise* God," my uncle Jorgi said, "the *whole* season is over. All the big, beautiful watermelons have been taken up and put in the *barn*."

"Your father will break your head," I said. "What will we do? The season is just beginning."

"It's ended," my uncle Jorgi said. "We will live in this house a month and then go home. We have paid six dollars for the house and we have money enough for rice. We will dream here a month and then go home."

My uncle Jorgi danced into the house to his zither. Before I could

---

"他自己，那个农场主自己说的，"乔奇叔叔说。

"他就是那么说说而已，"我说。"他们不想伤害你。他那么说就是因为知道你心不在焉。"

"赞美上帝吧，"乔奇叔叔说，"整个瓜季都结束了，所有那些大个儿的，漂亮的西瓜都已经摘完，放到仓库里了。"

"你老爸会敲碎你的脑袋，"我说。"咱们怎么办？瓜季才刚刚开始。"

"结束了，"乔奇叔叔说。"咱们就在这个房子里住上一个月，然后再回家。咱们付了六美元的房租，剩下的钱也足够买米。就在这儿自由自在地过上一个月再回家。"

乔奇叔叔手舞足蹈地进屋去拿齐特琴了。我还没想好该拿他怎么办，

---

praise *v.* 赞美；赞扬
barn *n.* 谷仓；仓房

whole *adj.* 整个的；完整的

decide what to do about him, he was playing and singing. It was beautiful. I didn't try to make him leave the house and go back to the farm. I just sat on the steps and listened.

We stayed in the house a month and then went home. My grandmother was the first to see us.

"You two came home just in time," she said. "He's been roaring like a tiger. Give me the money."

"There is no money," I said.

"Did he work?" my grandmother said.

"No," I said. "He played and sang the whole time."

"How was your rice?" she said.

"Sometimes salty," I said. "Sometimes swill. Sometimes *perfect*. But he didn't work."

---

他就已经弹唱起来。曲调很动听。我不想逼他离开这里回农场去。我干脆就坐在台阶上听他弹唱。

我们在那个房子里住了一个月，然后回家。祖母是第一个看到我们的。

"你们俩回来得正好，"她说。"你们走后，他总像个老虎似的整天吼叫。把钱给我。"

"没有钱，"我说。

"他干活了吗？"祖母问。

"没有，"我回答。"他一直都在弹唱。"

"你的饭做得怎么样？"

"有时咸，"我说。"有时像猪食，有时好吃极了。但是，他没干

---

perfect  *adj.*  完美的

"His father mustn't know," she said. "I have money."

She got some money out of a *pocket* and put it in my hands.

"When he comes home," she said, "give him this money."

"I will do as you say," I said.

When my grandfather came home he began to roar.

"Home already?" he said. "Is the season ended so soon? Where is the money he got?"

I gave him the money.

"I won't have him singing all day," my grandfather roared. "Some things simply have to stop, in the end. You will read in a book that a

---

活。"

"千万别让他老爸知道，"她说。"我这儿有钱。"

她从兜里拿出一些钱，放到我手里。说："他回来的时候，把钱给他。"

"我会照你说的去做，"我说。

祖父一回到家就开始吼叫。

"回来啦？"他说。"瓜季这么快就结束了？他挣的钱呢？"

我把钱递给他。

"我不会让他整天唱歌的，"祖父吼道。"有些事该停就得停。书里说有个当父亲的不偏爱聪明儿子，反倒偏爱傻儿子。说真的，那个写书的

---

pocket  *n.*  口袋

father loves a foolish son more than his wise sons. Believe me, that writer is not married, and also he has no sons."

In the yard, under the flowering tree, my uncle Jorgi began to play and sing. My grandfather came to a *dead* stop and began to listen. He sat down in his big chair, and began to make faces.

I went into the kitchen to get three or four glasses of water because of last night's rice. When I came back to the living room, the old man was sitting back in his chair, *asleep* and smiling. His son Jorgi was singing *praises* to the whole world at the top of his sad, beautiful voice.

---

肯定没结过婚，也没生过儿子。"

院子里，在开满鲜花的树下，乔奇叔叔又开始弹唱了。祖父顿时打住话头，凝神细听起来。他坐到那把大椅子上，又开始做鬼脸。

我去厨房弄了三四杯水——都怪昨晚的饭。当我回到客厅时，老头儿靠在椅子里睡着了，脸上还带着微笑。他的儿子乔奇正在用他那凄美的声音放声高歌全世界。

---

dead *adj.* 完全的；全然的  
praise *n.* 赞扬

asleep *adj.* 睡着的